Personification

Y

Personification discusses the theory behind multiplicity of the person and considers the implications that the relationships between the different parts of the same person have in practice. Providing both historical and contemporary insights John Rowan reveals new thinking and research in the field, as well as offering guidelines for using this information in practice.

The book also looks closely at the practice of personification – a technique involving the turning of a problem into a person and allowing a two-way dialogue through which the inner critic can be addressed and explored. As such, areas of discussion include:

- the use of multiplicity in therapy
- group work and the dialogical self
- the transpersonal.

This practical, straightforward book will be ideal reading for anyone using personification in their therapeutic work, including psychotherapists, counsellors and coaches.

John Rowan is a counsellor and psychotherapist, working with both individuals and couples, in private practice in north-east London. He is a Fellow of the British Association for Counselling and Psychotherapy and has an Honorary Fellowship from the UKCP. He is also a Fellow of the British Psychological Society and a founder member of the UK Association of Humanistic Psychology Practitioners.

Personification

Using the dialogical self in psychotherapy and counselling

John Rowan

Routledge
Taylor & Francis Group

LONDON AND NEW YORK

First published 2010
by Routledge
27 Church Road, Hove, East Sussex BN3 2FA

Simultaneously published in the USA and Canada
by Routledge
270 Madison Avenue, New York, NY 10016

Routledge is an imprint of the Taylor & Francis Group, an Informa business

Typeset in Times by Garfield Morgan, Swansea, West Glamorgan
Printed and bound in Great Britain by TJ International Ltd, Padstow,
Cornwall
Paperback cover design by Andrew Ward

British Library Cataloguing in Publication Data
A catalogue record for this book is available from the British Library

Library of Congress Cataloging-in-Publication Data
Rowan, John.
    Personification : using the dialogical self in psychotherapy and counselling /
John Rowan.
        p. cm.
    Includes bibliographical references and index.
    ISBN 978-0-415-43345-7 (hbk.) — ISBN 978-0-415-43346-4 (pbk.) 1. Self.
2. Personality. 3. Identity (Philosophical concept) I. Title.
    BF697.R677 2010
    155.2—dc22
                                                        2009026084

ISBN: 978-0-415-43345-7 (hbk)
ISBN: 978-0-415-43346-4 (pbk)

Contents

PART II
The dialogical self in therapy

Figures

Part I

Introduction

Introduction

This is a book which does three things:

a   It shows how important the idea of multiplicity within the person is to all psychotherapists, counsellors and coaches. We cannot understand people or work with them efficiently unless we understand that they are not simple creatures with just one will, just one outlook, just one set of wishes and needs. Within each person there are differing and sometimes conflicting desires.

   This puts the book in line with the recent academic thinking on constructivism, constructionism, postmodernism and so forth – though not with the more extreme expressions of this tendency. It helps to question notions like The Unconscious, The Denial of Death, The Real Self, The Organismic Tendency, The Collective Unconscious, The Brain, The Genital Character, The Anal Character, and so forth.

   The trouble with such notions is that they claim to be true. What we are doing in this book is to question the whole idea of one truth, one true belief, one answer to any psychological question. The answer is always multiple, always provisional, always questionable.

b   It explains how the basic idea of multiplicity within the person goes right back in history, and how it has been used in therapy in recent times. It is not a new idea, and it has been used in interesting and fruitful ways by a host of therapists of different persuasions – but all ignoring the others and therefore losing valuable inputs which it would be better to acknowledge and use.

   Many of them have made the mistake of simply saying that their version is right. Either the others are wrong or they are simply ignored. An enormous fault in the field of psychotherapy is ignorance of the person next door working in the same field, or active avoidance of any consideration of the others, or even rejection of the person next door.

   This puts the book in line with the passion I have always had about bridge-building. It hurts me to see the way in which writers in this field so strongly tend to quote only their own colleagues and friends, and to ignore parallel work in other fields. Freud talked about the "narcissism of small differences" and this is widely and wildly rampant in the field of psychotherapy. This book powerfully challenges that whole way of thinking.

c It gives a full account of the latest theory and research in the field, including a critique of some of the most popular ideas still being used at present. In particular, it critiques the concept of *subpersonalities*, saying that this concept lends itself too readily to reification and misplaced concreteness. It offers instead the notion of *I-positions*, developed and researched by a whole new school of theorists. The work of this school – the International Society for Dialogical Science – is explained and illustrated by examples. The connections between the dialogical self school and other recent developments – narrative therapy, assimilation theory, schema therapy and so forth – are also brought out and linked up.

This means that this book is up to date on what I believe to be the leading edge of solid scientific work in psychotherapy at present. It is a guide to a whole new world of discovery in the field. So what does this book do? It presents a comprehensive new way of making sense of personality and psychotherapy. It suggests substantial changes and advances. It links up with other challenging approaches to the work in a stimulating way. It is historically well founded, and goes on to break new ground.

But one important point to make is that all the way through, although the emphasis is clearly on technique, there is also a deep and consistent respect for, and understanding of, the relational approach. There is no contradiction between wanting to be real and relational and using effective techniques. The therapist is always an authentic trickster, and this paradoxical title is certainly adopted here. There is much more about this in Chapter 5.

There is also a secret desire behind the book. It is to try to influence the whole group of writers associated with the dialogical self. This is a movement started by Hubert Hermans in Nijmegen. He is a real polymath, having a wide knowledge of psychology and psychotherapy, and an extensive interest in the world beyond. He has made valuable links with researchers in Italy, Portugal, the USA, Poland, Brazil and many other countries – the 2008 international conference which he organized had people coming from 45 different lands.

My question to them is a simple one – why do you not use personification more in the actual therapy you conduct and research? The question goes to Giancarlo Dimaggio, William Stiles, Katerina Osatuke, Miguel Gonçalves, Jaan Valsiner, Paul Lysaker, Katarzyna Stemplewska-Zakowicz, João Salgado, and of course Hubert Hermans. Many others not mentioned know who they are.

But the main thrust of this book is to show everyone in the field of psychotherapy – not only those above – how useful is the idea of personification, and the concept of I-positions in relation to that. Hence I have felt it necessary to mention every field in which personification is used, and to critique it in the light of the new ideas. This gives both the positive introduction to each school and the essential critique to bring it into line with current theory. Thus much of this book may look familiar, but now each school is subjected to the insights developed in the light of dialogical self theory. This throws much new light on each one.

To put it another way, the historical material in the 1990 book on *Subpersonalities* seemed so well arranged and useful that it seemed pointless to research it all over again. People familiar with that book will therefore find much of the material in Chapter 4 is unchanged, though seen through another lens. In 1990 it was the scene in the morning light, so to speak, but now it is the same scene but in the evening light. It is certainly not unknown in other spheres such as painting and drama for the artist to return to a previous scene and see it afresh. So the old material has been revolutionized or "carnivalized" (Zizek) rather than rewritten. This then makes it possible to move on and into the new territories, having done justice to the old ones.

It is then possible to take the whole idea further, into the realm of the transpersonal. So long as we remain talking about ego states, subpersonalities, complexes and so forth, none of them leads us in the direction of the transpersonal – the spiritual, the divine, the numinous, the sacred, the holy. But as soon as we start using instead the notion of I-positions, it becomes possible to think in terms of talking to our soul, talking to our spirit, talking to God, talking to the Ultimate – and getting answers back! Because each of these can represent an I-position, and each of them can be talked to, and talk back. I used to think that the problem with prayer was that it was generally a one-sided conversation: I talked to God, but God never talked to me. Now that has all changed.

Of course, it is not all about God. Some of us prefer the Goddess anyway. But talking about Soul can take us deep inside the imaginal world of Henri Corbin, the world of the dreamweaver, the Underworld of James Hillman, and so forth. This level of insight is of course found in the various transpersonal schools, such as psychosynthesis, voice dialogue, some Jungians, the Almaas school and so forth. But here now is a demonstration that they need not be alone in their access to this rich and varied field. Now read on.

Chapter 1

A fresh look

In 1988 (published in 1990) I wrote a book entitled *Subpersonalities: The people inside us*. This was a pioneering effort, the first book to take such a concept and try to make all the connections that were required. It took until 1995 before any text on personality theory admitted that such things existed. Even now many of the main established texts do not mention such a thing. This book can be regarded as an extended critique of that pioneering text, because much has happened in the field since then.

In 1999 Mick Cooper and I co-edited a book called *The Plural Self: Multiplicity in everyday life*, which was a quantum leap forward from that. It included contributions from James Grotstein, Ruth-Inge Heinze, John Shotter, Alvin Mahrer, Brian Lancaster and particularly from Hubert Hermans. We were moving towards a realization that what was in the air was nothing less than a new theory of the human being, which reconciled the real multiplicity which is so obvious in the consulting room with the necessity for a self which undergoes all the vicissitudes of development from before conception to after death.

But it was not until the great international conference of 2008 that it became evident that what we had in the work of Hubert Hermans was nothing less than a reconciliation of the traditional view of the self, the modern view of the self and the postmodern view of the self. The traditional view gave us power relationships, agency and moral responsibility; the modern view gave us authenticity, choice and the existential edge; the postmodern view gave us the inclusion of all significant identifications, the decentring of the self, seeing the self as a linguistic construction and the questioning of all fixed positions. By taking up the notion of the dialogical self as a dynamic multiplicity of I-positions in the landscape of the mind we could resolve all this apparent antagonism and find something to live with.

People who have made the self into something single and simple still cannot grasp this, and struggle to see how the self can be multiple. They seem to think that having a single self is normal. But this means that they have to ignore the equally obvious truth that people are multiple. Who has not had the experience of being split? Who has not had the experience of enduring warring voices within? Perhaps it is the single self that has to be justified, in the face of the obvious multiplicity we encounter on all hands?

Years ago there was a big controversy in the pages of the *Journal of Humanistic Psychology* between the simplicity of Willard Frick (1993) and the multiplicity of James Fadiman (1993) and an attempt to heal the rift by Victor Bogart (1994), but the new thinking goes beyond this simple opposition by taking up quite a different standpoint.

The dialogical self

The new thinking comes from a number of different angles. The first and most prominent is the work of Hubert Hermans at Nijmegen University in the Netherlands. It was he who coined the term "the dialogical self". The fifth international conference on the dialogical self took place in 2008 in Cambridge. What he did was to shift the nomenclature from the older ideas of subselves, subpersonalities, ego states and so forth, all of which lent themselves to misunderstanding as solid entities all too easily, and introduce instead a new vocabulary based on I-positions.

> The notion of the "dialogical self" deviates from those associations and considers the self as a multiplicity of parts (voices, characters, positions) that have the potential of entertaining dialogical relationships with each other . . . The self functions as a society, being at the same time part of the broader society in which the self participates.
>
> (Hermans 2004, p.13)

Hermans and his colleagues, for example Giancarlo Dimaggio, Jaan Valsiner and Miguel Gonçalves, have conducted many research studies to explore their theory, and it is now well established, as we shall see in more detail later in this chapter.

What is remarkable, however, is that this is not the only approach which is now opening up the realm of multiplicity within the person. William Stiles, who goes back and forth between Ohio and Sheffield, has developed what he calls assimilation theory, which again has produced a large research programme to explore the idea of listening to the different voices which emerge during the course of therapy (Stiles & Glick 2002).

The person-centred school has in recent years begun to use the concept, under the heading of *configurations of self*, particularly in the hands of Dave Mearns and Mick Cooper. And this has enabled them to speak freely of the parts of the person which are negative.

> It is important that the person-centred therapist offer an equally full therapeutic relationship to *not for growth* configurations, like: "the 'me' that just wants to curl up and do absolutely nothing"; "the part that

wants to go back"; and "the bit of me that wants to destroy this therapist".

(Mearns & Thorne 2000, p.115)

This is quite a new departure for the person-centred school, and begins to sound much more like the psychoanalytic position about resistance.

Philip Bromberg, in the psychodynamic school, has made some very interesting points, showing that multiplicity is not at all foreign to that outlook.

> A noticeable shift has been taking place with regard to psychoanalytic understanding of the human mind and the nature of unconscious mental processes – away from the idea of a conscious/preconscious/unconscious distinction per se, towards a view of the self as decentered, and the mind as a configuration of shifting, nonlinear, discontinuous states of consciousness in an ongoing dialectic with the healthy illusion of unitary selfhood.
>
> (Bromberg 1998, p.xxxii)

Of course it is well known that Transactional Analysis and Gestalt therapy speak often of different parts of the person, but recently the torch has been taken up by experiential process therapy – much more interested in research than these earlier advocates.

> Process-experiential therapy has attempted to provide a comprehensive theory of treatment by integrating Gestalt and client-centered approaches. It combines the relationship conditions of empathy, prizing and congruence with more active interventions like empty-chair and two-chair work from Gestalt therapy, and focusing and evocative unfolding from Gendlin's and Rice's developments within client-centered therapy.
>
> (Watson et al. 1998, p.14)

The handbook edited by Leslie Greenberg and his collaborators (Greenberg et al. 1998) makes creative use of these ideas to intervene very effectively in research terms with people who have problems such as depression, post-traumatic stress, anxiety, psychosomatic disorders, sexual trauma, border-line personality disorder, dissociated and fragile process and so forth. This is exciting new work which needs to be better known.

And of course we must not forget the recent work in narrative therapy, based on the pioneers David Epston and Michael White at the Dulwich Centre in Adelaide. They and their collaborators (such as Michael Durrant and Cheryl White) have developed some fascinating ideas using personification to bring to life some important creatures, such as the Fear Monster,

Sneaky Wee, Sneaky Poo, Concentration, Tantrums, Misery, Guilt, Bad Habits, Zak (cannabis) and Sugar (diabetes). By working directly with such characters, they found that they could confirm the adage – "The person is not the problem. The problem is the problem." Jill Freedman and Gene Combs have added such I-positions as Bravery and Self-Blame (Freedman & Combs 1996).

Nor must we forget the recent work of Jeffrey Young and his collaborators in schema therapy. Their reseach has suggested that there are only 18 basic early maladaptive schemas, and only three modes of dealing with each one. This theory comes out of cognitive-behavioural therapy, and represents a much more sophisticated version of that basic outlook. "Schema therapists view experiential techniques as one of four equal components of treatment and devote considerable time in therapy to these strategies" (Young et al. 2003, pp.51–52). In a later discussion, the authors have this to say: "Patients learn to conduct dialogues between their 'schema side' and their 'healthy side'. Adapting the Gestalt 'empty chair' technique, the therapist instructs patients to switch chairs as they play the two sides: In one chair they play the schema side, in the other they play the healthy side" (p.100). This again is personification, and it seems clear that it fits well with the basic orientation.

If we listen carefully, we can begin to hear the emergence of different voices within the person. And armed with this new thinking, we can identify each voice as an I-position and treat it as such. There is then no problem about what status to give each voice – each one just represents another I-position. Ragnar Rommetveit is an eminent psychologist who pointed out some years ago that children are speaking in a dialogical way from the start. He says that "The human infant is, as far as mental development is concerned, dyadically embedded and dialogically operative. The developing human mind is hence dialogically constituted" (Rommetveit 1992, p.22). He goes on to say that adult verbal communication develops out of preverbal interaction between infant and adult caretaker as a dyadically structured and in some important sense circular activity. And this means that a distinctive and pervasive feature of the prototypical human discourse situation is thus a peculiar "attunement to the attunement of the other" (ibid.). This is well said, and it seems clear that this new thinking about the client is soundly based.

The research of Fogel and his colleagues on children in the first two years of life shows that "Each of the main features of the dialogical self – multiplicity of I-positions, embodiment of situated I-positions, and inter-subjectivity as constitutive of the dialogue between I-positions – can be observed in pre-verbal infants during communication frames" (Fogel et al. 2002, p.193). Although the infant is not yet able to use language, the interaction between mother and child is, without doubt, of a dialogical nature. The crucial point is that dialogue should not be restricted to verbal dialogue. In fact, much dialogue between people develops through body language, facial expression, smiling, gazing, vocalizations and intonations. Mead (1934) explicitly referred to the workings of gestures as central to his theory of symbolic interactionism, and even actions can be symbolically laden (e.g. punishing a child as an indication of disapproval). The conceptions of dialogue as comprising both verbal and nonverbal extends its relevance to cultural psychology as people from different cultures use both forms in their communication as part of their dialogical histories (Lyra 1999). (Similar points are made in Hermans 2001, pp.260–261.)

In fact, the work of Fogel is quite remarkable: the example is given in some detail of an infant playing with her mother, where after a normal sort of a game with a hand puppet operated by the mother, a sudden reversal takes place, showing clearly that the infant has grasped the idea of an I-position:

> Susan [17 months 2 weeks] and her mother have played the lion game many times in the past. In previous sessions, mother has always played the role of the agent, the lion (donning a lion hand puppet and roaring, scaring, tickling, etc.). Susan has always played the role of the recipient (being scared, being tickled, etc.). In this session, for the first time Susan tries to put the lion puppet on her own hand with the help of her mother and she activates it, as if to scare the mother.
>
> (Fogel et al. 2002, p.200)

Many of us have come across the situation where a child is punishing a teddy bear. We ask – "Why are you hitting the teddy bear?" The answer comes – "He's been very naughty!" If we then ask – "And what does the teddy bear say?" – we may well get an answer like – "He says he didn't do it!" This is striking stuff, and it all shows how simple and basic the idea of personification really is.

Of course the astute reader will have noticed that all this material is highly compatible with the basic case of constructionism, while avoiding the excesses of a one-sided postmodernism. The important book of G S Gregg put it very succinctly:

> The central point here is that the self consists not of a collection of Me attributions, as cognitive personality theorists would have it, nor of ego-syntonic identifications, as most psychoanalytic personality theories would have it, but of a system of Me/not-Me oppositions.
>
> (Gregg 1991, p.120)

Gregg pertinently asked the question as to how a unitary self, a single overarching system of symbols, could split felt experience, encode moral imperatives, and reconfigure itself according to the context. His answer was: very simply, in the same manner that a sentence can articulate *double entendre*, or a figure/ground illusion can switch between two pictures, or two notes an octave apart can be heard to be both the same and different.

As is well known, narrative therapy uses the idea very creatively and well. It often suggests personifying a problem to make it easier to handle. Instead of talking in terms of having a fear, the client is encouraged to think of the fear as a person who is trying to dominate. Then we can talk to the Fear and get the Fear to talk back, as Jill Freedman and Gene Combs have shown in some detail (Freedman & Combs 1996).

White and Epston powerfully influenced the Dulwich Centre in New Zealand, and these people have produced a number of papers along these lines. Barbara Wingard has a very interesting one showing how a group can engage with diabetes, by giving diabetes a name (Sugar) and letting it be interrogated by the group (Wingard 1998). A group of writers set up a very valuable group interaction about cannabis (in New Zealand often known as Dak) by personifying Dak and letting him interact from direct knowledge (Cronin-Lampe et al. 1999).

Since then narrative therapy has developed and burgeoned, as John McLeod (1997) has spelt out in detail. However, the idea of personification was not well researched by these people, who used the idea rather informally though persuasively. This was still so in the very exciting book by Jill Freedman and Gene Combs (1996) which made links with social constructionism. We shall return to narrative therapy in a later chapter.

Going deeper

In 1992 Hubert Hermans at the University of Nijmegen instigated a new literature of the dialogical self, based on the philosophy of Bakhtin and Voloshinov:

> In his book *Problems of Dostoevsky's Poetics* (1929/1973), the Russian literary scholar Mikhail Bakhtin argued that Dostoevsky – a brilliant innovator in the realm of literary form – created a peculiar type of artistic thought, the "polyphonic novel". Central to Bakhtin's thesis is the idea that in Dostoevsky's works there is not a single author at work – Dostoevsky himself – but *several* authors or thinkers – characters such as Raskolnikov, Myshkin, Stavrogin, Ivan Karamazov, and the Grand Inquisitor. Instead of being obedient slaves of the one author, Dostoevsky, each of these heroes is ideologically authoritative and independent and uses his own voice to ventilate his view and philosophy. Each hero is perceived as the author of his own ideology, and not as the object of Dostoevsky's finalizing artistic vision. There is not a

multitude of characters and fates within a unified objective world, organized by Dostoevsky's individual consciousness, but a plurality of consciousnesses and worlds.

(Hermans 1992, p.73)

Hermans is a careful scholar with access to good research facilities, who also quotes William James as a precursor of these ideas. But Bakhtin (an important writer in his own right) is his primary inspiration:

In Bakhtin's (1929/1973) terms, "The plurality of independent unmerged voices and consciousnesses and the genuine polyphony of full-valued voices are in fact characteristics of Dostoevsky's novels" (p.4). As in a polyphonic musical work, multiple voices accompany and oppose one another in a dialogical way. For Bakhtin, agreement and disagreement are, like question and answer, basic dialogical forms.

The notion of dialogue enabled Dostoevsky to express a character's inner world and articulate a character's personality. As soon as a neutral utterance is attributed to a particular character, dialogical relations may spontaneously occur between this utterance and the utterances of another character. For example, in Dostoevsky's novel *The Double,* the second hero (the double) was introduced as a personification of the interior voice of the first hero (Golyadkin). In this way the interior voice is externalized, and a dialogue between two independent parties is allowed to develop, where each character – as an independent author – can tell a story about himself. As a result of a process of exchange, the stories are not only differentiated and contrasted but also further developed.

(Hermans 1992, p.74)

As Hermans went on to expand on his basic insight, he brought in other scholars, notably Giancarlo Dimaggio in Rome. Dimaggio is responsible for a good deal of research on the dialogical self, particularly in relation to psychotherapy. He says:

DST [Dialogical Self Theory] is a narrative theory (Bruner 1986; Sarbin 1986), based on the idea that the stories we tell ourselves give meaning to and anticipate events, provide for action planning, consolidate our self-understanding, establish our characteristic range of emotions and life goals, and guide our performance on the social world stage (Neimeyer 2004). Within the stories one can note different characters interacting. Each is equivalent to a facet of the self and is able to take centre stage, become the protagonist of the story and speak with its own authorial voice, to take decisions and guide the overall action of the individual . . . Identity is not, therefore, based on the decisions of a central and omniscient ego but arises from the constant dialogue between *characters* (Bakhtin 1929/1973), known also as *voices*, *positions*, *sub-personalities* or *roles*, endowed with agent-like qualities (Stiles 1999). Each character can be described as a cluster of personal constructs (Kelly 1955/1991a,b; Hermans 1996). From this perspective, therefore, the self is portrayed as being multiple . . . The different voices have the potential of entertaining dialogical relationships with each other and of being involved in communicative interchange (Hermans 2003). They literally *speak* with each other and it is through this dialogue, which can occur in one's imaginal internal space or with others in daily life, that one ascribes meaning to events.

(Dimaggio et al. 2007)

One of the main proposals of the present text is that dialogical self theory offers a sound and well-researched improvement on earlier ideas.

Jaan Valsiner has made the important point that

The dialogical self entails two domains – intra-psychological and inter-psychological – both of which are equally important. A person operates on the basis of two dialogical processes: *heterodialogue* (with others, including imaginary others) and *autodialogue* (within oneself). In fact, these two dialogues are mutually intertwined. A person who tries to state something to a listener is simultaneously hearing (or reading) his or her own statement, which becomes part of the auto-dialogical process, irrespective of any answer from the listener.

(Valsiner 2002, p.252)

This is something worth keeping in mind throughout.

Dialogical self theory

Hermans (1992) conceptualized the self in terms of a dynamic multiplicity of relatively autonomous I-positions in the landscape of the mind. A few years later a more elaborate formulation put it this way:

Dialogical Self Theory considers the self as a multiplicity of parts (voices, characters, positions) that have the potential of entertaining dialogical relationships with each other . . . the different parts of the self are not only involved in communicative interchange, they are also subjected to relative dominance, with some parts being more powerful or speaking with a louder voice than other parts . . . the dialogical self . . . is based on the assumption that the processes that are taking place

> between the different parts of the self are also taking place in the relationship between the individual and him- or herself. The self functions as a society.
>
> (Hermans 2004, p.13)

Dialogical self theory is grounded in narrative theory (Angus & McLeod 2004; Bruner 1990), the idea of which is that the stories we tell ourselves give meaning to and anticipate events, provide for action planning, consolidate our self-understanding, establish our characteristic range of emotions and goals, and guide our performance on the stage of the social world (Neimeyer 2000). Stories contain various characters, each equivalent to a facet of self. Some of these characters are the authors of the stories, the self-as-subject (I) in James' terms; others are talked about, and correspond to the self-as-object (Me); others may comment on the stories told in this way, and so may occupy a meta-position which is self-reflexive.

Identity is not, therefore, based on the decisions of a central and omniscient ego but surfaces from the constant dialogue between aspects of the self given agent-like-qualities, which may be called voices (Stiles 1999), characters (Bruner 1990), subpersonalities (Rowan 1990), I-positions (Hermans 2004), possible selves (Dunkel & Kerpelman 2006), personas (Bogart 2007) or roles (Horowitz 1987; Ryle & Kerr 2002). Each one of them represents a point of view in relation to the others, for example, the protective voice of the father of a little girl may get replaced by a competitive voice typical of an animated discussion with a work colleague.

The different parts of a multiple self are involved in communicative interchange, which takes the form of a dialogue (Angus & McLeod 2004; Hermans 1996; Lysaker & Lysaker 2004) in which each voice may be in accord or discord with the other. For example, a man may be divided, one I-position wishing to spend the weekend with his children and another wishing to complete an important piece of work. The dialogical self is based on the assumption that we can profitably speak of processes that are taking place between the different parts of the self, or in the relationship between the individual and him- or herself. The internal dialogue may take the form of a critical parent (Berne 1961) as against a nurturing parent, in trying to make a decision, such as for example to go on holiday (Hermans 2004). The voice may come across as some aspect of myself (myself as a mediocre father, an enthusiastic darts player, etc.), or perhaps someone else who has the required characteristics. Or it may take the form of a persecutor, or a victim, or a rescuer – or even a bystander (Clarkson 1992) – whatever character it may take to play the role, or, as we could also say, take over the I-position (Greenberg 2002; Hermans 1996; Hermans & Dimaggio 2004). The meaning of events emerges from the form that the dialogue takes. Finally, some of the voices may be consistently submerged or surface only rarely (Bakhtin 1927/1973; Leiman & Stiles 2001; Hermans 1996; Hermans

& Dimaggio 2004). For example, a strong character may be the dominant one in narratives and the weak and needy part surfaces with difficulty, which makes it impossible for the subject to ask for help and obtain it.

The characters often assume positions that are different and contradictory. To give an impression of unity and integration an individual needs to develop self-reflexive points of view that take account of these differences and create self-narratives that explain them ("I'm an unfaithful husband, but I'd never do any harm to my wife and I protect her when necessary"). There are various names for this self-observing point of view: reflexive function (Fonagy & Target 1996), metacognitive or metarepresentative skills (Sperber 2000; Semerari et al. 2003), meta-position (a character, that is, which observes other characters' actions, Hermans 2003) and observing-I (Leiman & Stiles 2001).

What is consistent in all this is a refusal to reify the I-positions, as is done in the theories of ego-states, subpersonalities, subselves and so forth. We do not look upon them as homunculi inside the person, but as responses to a situation, and only valid within that situation. We do not worry whether the same response may arise over and over again: we just deal with it in the moment. This makes it much easier to let it transform and move on when that is indicated. We do not envisage it as a fixed entity that may resist change, but as a momentary position that comes and goes.

In the years since 1992, much work has been done, as can be seen from the number of references in the last few paragraphs. We shall come back to this school later, as the research they have done on the actual process of therapy is very important. There have now been several international conferences and a journal has been launched. In 2004 this resulted in the publication of a major text edited by Hermans, featuring many new writers who had taken up this way of seeing the world.

Assimilation theory

In 1998 William Stiles and Lara Honos-Webb began to publish a series of studies under the banner of assimilation theory, showing through research that in a therapy session it is quite normal for the same person to speak in a number of voices, representing different parts of themselves.

> The *assimilation model* is an empirically researched account of psychotherapy process, focusing on stages of clients' change. According to the model, traces of a person's experiences are manifested as agentic internal *voices*, and personality is understood as a community of such voices . . . We introduce the notion of *subcommunities of voices*, i.e. constellations of voices that appear unassimilated to each other. They are manifested as drastic shifts in self-states and availability of personal resources. We propose five distinctions and illustrate them with clinical

> examples: Voices or subcommunities (1) may be dominant or non-dominant and (2) included in a community to different degrees. They (3) may express broader or more limited segments of experience, which (4) may be processed more or less thoroughly. Finally, (5) they may be avoided or engaged by the community to varying degrees.
>
> (Osatuke & Stiles 2006)

The authors go on to say that the concept of multiple self is particularly friendly to constructivist approaches, with their interest in multiple perspectives and their view of psychological structures as emerging from interactions of a multi-levels organism-environment system.

They have developed a theory of voices which allows for the possibility that a therapist could help to construct a meaning bridge between client and therapist that enables the client's internal voices to communicate with each other and even engage in joint action (Stiles & Glick 2002).

As we shall see in more detail later, this work entails that the therapist learn a form of family therapy, enabling each voice to be heard and taken into account.

> As respect and empathy are offered to each voice individually, conflicting internal voices can hear and come to respect each other, a crucial step on the way to developing internal meaning bridges. To implement this position, we suggest that, in hearing conflicting expressions, therapy might better reflect one voice at a time, which we call *univocal reflection*, rather than try to encompass multiple voices in an omnibus reflection.
>
> (Stiles & Glick 2002, p.409)

This idea was of course also found in the earlier work of Beahrs (1982) who also made the link with family therapy.

But the Stiles work is so recent that at the time of writing there is no complete text dealing with the theory, although many individual papers have been published.

In 2001 Eugenie Georgaca published a theoretically sophisticated paper bringing together ideas from Bakhtin and from Lacan to suggest that the self is plural, consisting of a multiplicity of positions, voices, states of mind and so forth.

In 2003 appeared the massive text from Jeffrey Young and his co-workers explaining the theory and practice of schema therapy, developed over a period of years since its first beginnings in cognitive therapy in 1990. This is a brilliant book, which would be of real interest to any therapy practitioner. Schema therapy comes from the cognitive-behavioural camp, and is strongly research based: it includes two-chair work and the use of imagery and mindfulness meditation.

It says that there are basically 18 things that can go wrong in childhood, which the authors call Early Maladaptive Schemas. Those who are up with the relevant literature will know that schemas have been growing in popularity as important psychological concepts recently. The beauty of a schema is that it is of the same basic nature as a subpersonality, an archetype, an ego state, a deeper potential – in other words, something that can be personified. Anything that can be personified can be dialogued with and understood from the inside.

It goes on to say that given one of these schemas, there are basically only three reactions one can have to it: surrender, avoidance or compensation.

Because this is a book for practitioners, there are heaps of examples, shorter or longer bursts of dialogue between client and therapist, some of which are very moving. One of the things I admire most about this book is the way in which it says that therapists also may have Early Maladaptive Schemas, some of which may not have been worked through and dealt with in any thorough way in their own therapy. There is often a possibility, therefore, of a mismatch, where the client's schema triggers off something in the therapist's own schema which is unhelpful or deleterious. This is a good point to make, and it would be good if more practitioner texts made this clear.

> A crucial difference between the two approaches (CBT and schema therapy) is in the importance of experiential work, such as imagery and dialogues . . . Schema therapists view experiential techniques as one of four equal components of treatment and devote considerable time in therapy to these strategies . . . Experiential techniques can sometimes be the only way to stimulate hot cognitions in the session.
>
> (Young et al. 2003, pp.51–52)

This is a very important point because it is generally accepted in the cognitive literature that 'hot cognitions' (when the client is experiencing strong feelings) can be changed more readily than 'cold cognitions' (when the client's feelings are flat).

The authors take on the whole range of problems which people may bring to therapists, and have found that with the more difficult syndromes – Borderline Personality Disorder and Narcissistic Personality Disorder – they have to move into what they call a Schema Mode approach. This simply treats a group of schemas as one, depending on the actual actions and interactions of the client. It does offer answers, and also a host of ways of arriving at answers, designed to help the therapist who may be in difficulties. There are many hints and tips on how to handle difficult clients, which make a lot of sense.

Directly on the question of personification, the authors say – "Adapting the Gestalt 'empty chair' technique, the therapist instructs patients to switch chairs as they play the two sides: In one chair they play the schema side, in the other they play the healthy side" (Young et al. 2003, p.100). The authors say: "It has been our experience that there are fundamental differences in effective change techniques for symptom reduction compared with personality change" – and they are more interested in the latter. This is why they are so interested in imagery and dialogues, both of which encourage "hot cognitions" – so important in real transformation. The schema therapist sometimes engages in battle with the schema rather than sympathizing with it all the time.

And in 2004 appeared the striking paper by Avants and Margolin, in which they argue for the use of the idea of a spiritual self-schema in dealing with addiction.

We shall be meeting all these people and their ideas in the pages to come, but already it seems obvious that much has been going on in the general area of multiplicity within the person.

We all use the concept in our folk psychology, but until recently it had escaped the notice of orthodox academic personality theory. What I want to argue is that academic personality theory is going to have to take notice of it in the future.

It is obviously convenient for someone trying to construct a personality test to assume that there is just one personality. But that is all it is – an assumption, a convenience. It would be more inconvenient if we had to admit that people could have one personality in one frame, and another in another. The whole idea of a personality test might have to change.

So this book is partly addressed to psychologists working in the field of personality, and of the self, and of identity – all those kinds of questions.

It is also addressed to psychotherapists, encouraging them to look outside the walls of their training institutes at what is going on elsewhere to deal with the self-same problems as they are tackling themselves. There is a lot of talk about the therapeutic relationship nowadays, but what about the internal relationships – what about the relationships between different parts of the same person?

It is also addressed to the general reader, who would like to know how brilliant people can be in this field, and how stupid. For anyone just interested in human beings (including people working in the human sciences) and how they function and act, this book is full of illuminating examples and accounts.

Chapter 2

Implications

The implication I want to draw out from all this ferment is that there can now be a new rapprochement between the different schools within psychology.

Cognitive psychology can have no difficulty in admitting the notion of a dialogical self, since they have no particular theory of the self that could interfere with its acceptance. The cognitive therapist has therefore no basis for denying the value of seeing the person as multiple rather than single.

Humanistic psychology has no difficulty at all: Psychodrama has always assumed that various parts of the person can be personified and communicated with; Gestalt specialized in the use of two-chair experiments of various kinds; more recently the person-centred approach has also begun to see the value of postulating "configurations of self" as helping in the process of therapy.

Psychoanalysis has become much more varied in recent years, with the old dogmatic tendencies having been severely diminished. So we now find someone like Philip Bromberg saying things like this:

> In a book entitled *More Than Human,* written in 1953, Theodore Sturgeon, one of the most creative and visionary science fiction authors of the twentieth century, wrote the following: "Multiplicity is our first characteristic; unity our second. As your parts know they are parts of you, so must you know that we are parts of humanity" (p.232). I think it might be interesting to allow Sturgeon's words to remain in your mind, but to now let yourself hear them in the context of a not dissimilar viewpoint offered by someone seemingly unlike Sturgeon, at least in any obvious way – a classical psychoanalyst whose sensibility is more pragmatic than visionary, and whose "professional self," at least in most of her writing, has embodied a traditionally positivistic approach to the nature of reality. In a paper in the *Psychoanalytic Quarterly,* Janine Lampl-de Groot (1981) reported being so persuaded by the power of the clinical evidence supporting multiplicity of selfhood, that she advanced the then extraordinary hypothesis that the

phenomenon of multiple personality is present in all human beings as a basic phenomenon of mental functioning. Whether or not one agrees with her use of terminology, I think it is fair to say that an increasing number of contemporary analysts now share the clinical observations that led her to this conclusion – that even in the most well-functioning individual, normal personality structure is shaped by dissociation as well as by repression and intrapsychic conflict.

(Bromberg 1998, p.270)

Not only is Bromberg here embracing the notion of multiplicity as such, but he goes on to say that such a notion is useful in the process of psychoanalysis itself:

Parallel with this development, a noticeable shift has been taking place with regard to psychoanalytic understanding of the human mind and the nature of unconscious mental processes – away from the idea of a conscious/preconscious/unconscious distinction per se, towards a view of the self as decentered, and the mind as a configuration of shifting, nonlinear, discontinuous states of consciousness in an ongoing dialectic with the healthy illusion of unitary selfhood. Sherry Turkle (1978), for example, sees Lacan's focus on the decenteredness of selfhood as his most seminal contribution, and writes that "for generations, people have argued about what was revolutionary in Freud's theory and the debate has usually centered on Freud's ideas about sexuality. But Lacan's work underscores that part of Freud's work that is revolutionary for our time. The individual is 'decentered.' There is no autonomous self" (p.xxxii).

(Bromberg 1998, pp.270–271)

What we have here is a remarkable rapprochement between very different historical traditions in psychology.

The developmental story

Of course one of the major traditions in psychology is developmental psychology, and here a great deal of the newer research is coming up with the notion of multiplicity as normal and natural in the young child. Young children do not have to be taught that they are multiple: they talk to themselves as a matter of course, correcting themselves, arguing with themselves, congratulating themselves and so forth.

Now, if the newborn's mind could be specified in a self-organising system that recreates and transforms itself in immediate mutual engagements with actual others, then a path would open for a tentative reply. This is the explanatory path proposed:

- An inner, primary companion process (and space for dialoguing), termed "the virtual other" inviting and permitting replacement by actual others, is postulated as inherent in the operational circuits by which the mind recreates and transforms itself.
- This permits the mind, even that of the newborn, to be operationally specified as a self-organizing dyad whether realized (i) in the individual (with the virtual other) or (ii) between individuals (with actual others).
- Actual others who replace the virtual other are felt in presentational immediacy (felt immediacy).
- Hence, when states and circumstances permit, infant-adult dyads are expected to exhibit protodialogue and other patterns indicative of mutual affect attunement.

(Braten 1992, p.80)

These are not odd findings from the periphery: they are important insights emerging again and again in different research programmes. The well-known social psychologist Ragnar Rommetveit, after making some more basic points, has this to say:

(8) The human infant is, as far as mental development is concerned, dyadically embedded and dialogically operative.
(9) The developing human mind is hence dialogically constituted.
(10) Adult verbal communication develops out of preverbal interaction between infant and adult caretaker as a dyadically structured and in some important sense circular activity.
(11) A distinctive and pervasive feature of the prototypical human discourse situation is thus a peculiar "attunement to the attunement of the other".

(Rommetveit 1992, p.22)

How familiar to any parent is the scene where the very young child is punishing the teddy bear, and the parent says – "Why are you doing that?" – and the child says – "Teddy has been naughty" – and the parent says – "And what does Teddy say?" – and the child says – "He says he didn't do it." We are dialogic from the very first.

The importance of I-positions

How different psychology would be if we all took these points for granted in our own lives and works. Most of us have had the experience of being "taken over" by a part of ourselves which we didn't know was there. We say – "I don't know what got into me." This is generally a negative experience, although it can be positive too. The way in which we usually recognize the presence of a different voice is that we find ourselves, in a particular situation, acting in ways which we do not like or which go against our interests, and unable to change this by an act of will or a conscious decision. This lasts as long as the situation lasts – perhaps a few minutes, perhaps an hour, perhaps a few hours – and then it changes by itself when we leave this situation and go into a different one. As long as 30 years ago it was possible for a good and quite uncontroversial text on social psychology (Middlebrook 1974) to say things like – "Thus the individual is not a single self, but many selves, which change somewhat as the individual shifts from situation to situation and person to person. We are, in short, what the situation demands."

The question of whether there are parts of a person which can be talked to and worked with as if they were separate little personalities with a will of their own is one which has fascinated nearly everyone who has had to work with people in any depth. Phrases like – "On the one hand I want to . . . on the other hand I don't", "I don't know how I could have done it", "It was as if a voice was telling me off" – are so common that they inevitably give a counsellor or therapist the cue that more than one system is at work. Internalized mothers and fathers are so common that it has almost become a joke. All these are examples of ways in which the idea of a dialogical person presents itself very patently and obviously.

But what is the right definition of such parts? I spent some time in the 1980s trying to find one. I found six or seven different definitions, and then added one of my own. But then it seemed that none of this would do. I was trying to find a definition of something which was too wide-ranging, too disparate, to yield to a single definition, no matter how ingenious. Regard the problem: how to reconcile the Freud (1923) who wrote of the ego, the id and the superego; the Jung (1928) who talked about the complexes or the archetypes; the Federn (1952) or Berne (1961) or John Watkins (1978b) who spoke of ego states; the Lewin (1936) who wrote about subregions of the personality; the Perls (1951) who referred to the topdog and the underdog, or retroflection; the Klein (1948) or Fairbairn (1952) or Guntrip (1971) who talked about internal objects; the Balint (1968) who delineated the child in the patient; the Mary Watkins (1986) who described imaginal objects, such as the imaginary friend; the McAdams (1985) who deployed the concept of imagoes as a key to life histories; the Hilgard (1986) who discovered the "hidden observer" in hypnotic states; the Tart (1986) who spoke of identity states; the Denzin (1987) who talked about the emotionally divided self; the Winnicott (1965) or Lake (1966) or Janov (1970) or Laing (1976) who referred to the false or unreal self; the Gurdjieff (1950) who introduced the concept of little I's; the Goffman (1974) who referred to multiple selfing; the Stone and Winkelman (1985) who used the concept of energy patterns; the Mahrer (1978) who theorized deeper potentials coming to the surface; the Mair (1977) who opened up the possibility of a community of self; the Ornstein (1986) who spoke of small minds; the Gazzaniga (1985) or Minsky (1988) who discovered agents and agencies within the brain; the Gergen (1972) or Martindale (1980) or O'Connor (1971) or Shapiro (1976) who refer to subselves; the Strauss or Rossan who talk about subidentities; the Markus and Nurius (1987) who speak of possible selves; the Kihlstrom and Cantor (1984) who introduce the concept of self-schemas; the Bogart (2007) who speaks of personas; the Mearns and Thorne (2000) who speak of the configurations of self; the T B Rogers (1981) who writes about prototypes; the Beahrs (1982) who refers to alter-personalities, or the Assagioli (1975) or Redfearn (1985) or Sliker (1992) who talk about subpersonalities – all the time we are talking about the same thing – this thing which is not mentioned in the major textbooks of personality.

More recently, as we have already seen, there has been a move towards assimilating the idea of subpersonalities into the dialogical model of the person originally put forward by Bakhtin (1981) and Voloshinov (1986). People like John Shotter (1999) and Hubert Hermans (1999) have led the way into the work of people like Philip Bromberg (2004) and others. This is a research-based approach, which puts forward a well developed conception of the person as engaged in dialogues not only external but also internal. This takes the whole idea into a new arena which is far more unified – perhaps at the expense of making the links with other disciplines which I personally find so valuable. This is a much more philosophical approach as well, taking the trouble to give a sound basis to the research.

A further innovation in recent years has been the introduction of the 'assimilation model' of William Stiles and others. An interesting example of this work is to be found in Honos-Webb et al. (1999), following the therapeutic work of one client, and distinguishing between the different versions of her which emerged during the course of the therapy. More recently, Osatuke et al. (2005) have gone through the therapy of one person, just considering the voice quality, and found six subsystems of the person, each with a different voice. This again is serious research, throwing another new light on to the question of multiplicity within the person.

And one of the most interesting developments in recent years is the coming of narrative therapy (White & Epston 1990). This follows Foucault's idea that we are often living out other people's stories about us, and sees the object of therapy as beginning to own and create our own stories. In doing this it is often valuable to personalize our problems and confront them as if they were separate persons. This "challenges the techniques that subjugate persons to a dominant ideology" (p.29). And these ideas have been built on further by people like Jill Freedman and Gene Combs (1996).

The new freedom

I am therefore now proposing that we drop all attempts to produce neat definitions, and instead look at the whole phenomenon from the standpoint of psychotherapy. From this position all we need to say is that we can make use of: "Any aspect of the person which can be personified." Instead of trying to found the phenomenon on philosophy or on particular practices or insights, we simply say that in psychotherapy it is often useful to personify aspects of the person, so that the client can interact with them as if they were people, or allow them to interact with each other as if they were people. For some good examples of how this can be done see the moving book by Fritz Perls (1969), for a full discussion of using this approach in practice see Cooper and Cruthers (1999), and for some good research on the practice of methods like this see Strümpfel and Goldman (2002).

This is really a huge step forward, which makes the whole set of questions around subpersonalities irrelevant. No longer do we have to ask where they come from, how many of them there are, whether they really exist or not, what their ontological status is, whether they should be given names or not, and so forth – all that goes by the board. Instead, we simply ask in each case – is it useful to treat this as if it were a person, or not?

The view from cultural psychology is that here, again, we have to take real multiplicity into account:

> A voice can contain a reference to the label of the collectivities a person *feels* (rather than formally is) connected with (e.g. I as a psychologist, a woman or a German). Notice here that the label of a voice is not the voice itself: my "I as a psychologist" voice is probably different from your "I as a psychologist" voice. Thus, naming the voice by a *social role label* (psychologist) does not say anything about its *personal meaning*. A voice can also be idiosyncratic in nature (I as an adventurer, a dreamer or a witch). A voice can also be a reconstruction of another "real" person's voice (the voice of my mother, the voice of someone deceased [Josephs 1998]) or a construction of an "imaginal" figure (the voice of my imaginal friend [Watkins 1986]). It can be related to belief-systems (the voice of God), or to symbolic-material aspects of our worlds (the voice of a precious object [Fuhrer & Josephs 1999], the voice of a cultural symbol [Hermans & van Loon 1991]).
>
> (Josephs 2002, p.162)

Marie-Louise von Franz has suggested in an interview on film that one can be very free in this work:

> I could give you a whole list of the persons I can be. I am an old peasant woman who thinks of cooking and of the house. I am a scholar who thinks about deciphering manuscripts. I am a psychotherapist who

thinks about how to interpret people's dreams. I am a mischievous little boy who enjoys the company of a ten-year-old and playing mischievous tricks on adults, and so on. I could give you twenty more such characters. They suddenly enter you, but if you see what is happening you can keep them out of your system, play with them and put them aside again. But if you are possessed, they enter you involuntarily and you act them out involuntarily.

(Boa 1988, p.241)

The point for now is that we are not dealing with multiple personality, or any kind of dissociative disorder. We do not have to worry about the precise relationship between ordinary subpersonalities and dissociative disorders, because we are not talking about subpersonalities now.

I do not want to give the impression that the new thinking has supplanted all the older ideas in the field. A deep thinker like Hillman, who has been talking about personification for many years, still has much to teach us. Archetypal psychology extends Jung's personified naming of the components of personality – shadow, anima, animus, trickster, old wise man, great mother, etc. Personifying or imagining things becomes crucial for moving from an abstract, objectified psychology to one that encourages animistic engagement with the world. Personifying further allows the multiplicity of psychic phenomena to be experienced as voices, faces, and names. Psychic phenomena can then be perceived with precision and particularity. James Hillman argues strongly for such ideas in the striking chapter entitled "Personifying or imagining things" in his book on re-visioning psychology (Hillman 1975, pp.1–51).

These are very important ideas, and it is not the intention at all to downgrade or forget about thoughts like this. Rather is there an immense respect for the early pioneers who have given us so much. And just because many of the new researchers do not mention the soul, it is all the more important to keep alive the views of those who do. Hillman goes on to say:

For archetypal psychology, consciousness is given with the various "partial" personalities. Rather than being imagined as split-off fragments of the "I," they are better reverted to the differentiated models of earlier psychologies where the complexes would have been called souls, daimones, genii, and other mythical-imaginal figures. The consciousness that is postulated a priori with these figures or personifications is demonstrated by their interventions in ego control, i.e., the psychopathology of everyday life (Freud), disturbances of attention in the association experiments (Jung), the willfulness and aims of figures in dreams, the obsessive moods and compulsive thoughts that may intrude during any *abaissment du niveau mental* (Janet). Whereas most psychologies attempt to ban these personalities as disintegrative, archetypal psychology favors bringing non-ego figures to further awareness and considers this tension with the non-ego which relativizes the ego's surety and single perspective to be a chief occupation of soul-making.

(Hillman 1983, pp.52–53)

Let us therefore go back and pick up some of the history that is relevant here.

History

It is not easy to discover the history of the idea of the dialogical self. It is one of those concepts, so common in the field of the human sciences, which has a long past but a short history.

Most primitive cultures, both ancient and modern, have been aware of altered states of consciousness and spirit possession, both of which are forerunners. Priests, witchdoctors and shamans have made these ideas a stock in trade since early in the history of the human race. There were "sleep temples" in ancient Greece and in Egypt where patients were encouraged to go into altered states of consciousness, were actually hypnotized or were talked to during their sleep and given curative suggestions. Gods and goddesses, as we shall see later, can sometimes usefully be thought of as projected I-positions. The Druids, the Celtic priesthood, are supposed to have been experts in the use of these methods. In primitive cultures, these changes have often been brought about through the use of trances, and trance induction has been brought about by means of rhythm, drums, dancing, chanting, etc.

The earliest example I have come across of someone actually talking to an internal person, and being answered back, comes in an Egyptian document of approximately 2200 BC – a dialogue between a suicidal man and his soul. This is quoted in full and explained at length by Barbara Hannah (1981), who makes some very interesting comments on it.

In *The Republic*, Plato speaks of three parts to the psyche: the rational, the appetitive (concerned with bodily needs such as hunger and thirst), and the spirited one. In the *Phaedrus* he speaks more concretely of a three-part psyche, imaged as a charioteer and two horses. One horse is a lover of honour, modesty and temperance, who seems to be prudent and restrained; the other a crooked, lumbering animal with insolence, pride and impulsiveness, who seems very much the voice of instinct.

Many later thinkers had different versions of this type of approach, and in the Middle Ages we find this sort of thing:

The problem of the unity of personality had already been pondered over by St Augustine in his Confessions. Considering the change that had taken place in him since his conversion, Augustine remarked that his old pagan personality, of which nothing seemed to remain in his waking state, still must exist since it was revived at night and in his dreams. He wrote: "Am I not myself, O Lord, my God. And yet, there is so much difference between myself and myself within the moment wherein I pass from waking to sleeping or return from sleeping to waking." This brings Augustine to discuss the problem of the dreamer's moral responsibility for his dreams. Later the analogous problem of the individual's responsibility for actions committed by his "secondary personality" would become the subject of similar investigation.

(Ellenberger 1970, p.147)

Augustine also emphasized the fact that memories from early infancy, which we had thought to be entirely lost, can reappear, and that our brains retain traces of all that we have previously experienced.

Barbara Hannah (1981) also gives us a very full example of a twelfth-century dialogue with the soul, coming from Hugh de St Victor. And she points to a quotation of Jung from the early Church father Origen – "You will see that a man who seems to be one is not one, but as many different persons appear in him as he has attitudes" (Jung 1946, p.197).

Similarly, in this book we are not much concerned with hypnosis, but it is a fact that the unconscious was explored by hypnotists (mesmerists, magnetizers, etc.) for 150 years or so before psychotherapy as we know it came on the scene.

As has been pointed out by Carlson (1986), the concept of the unconscious had to come first, and the concept of dual personality actually came very early. We can even pinpoint a year (1784) when the idea of the unconscious came into the sphere of psychology, through the work of the Comte de Puységur (Chertok & de Saussure 1979).

At the start of the nineteenth century, the philosopher Herbart (with whose work Freud was well acquainted) was already talking about the psychology of internal conflict, the unconscious and repression.

All through the nineteenth century was growing up what Henri Ellenberger calls the first dynamic psychiatry. In this body of work:

a new model of the human mind was evolved. It was based on the duality of conscious and unconscious psychism. Later, it was modified to the form of a cluster of subpersonalities underlying the conscious personality . . . In the latter part of the nineteenth century the concepts of the autonomous activity of split fragments of personality and of the mythopoetic function of the unconscious arose.

(Ellenberger 1970, p.111)

We shall see later how the mythopoetic function is very central to what we are talking about in this book. So it is worthwhile to take notice of what

Ellenberger says about this important aspect of the unconscious and its working.

> The mythopoetic function (a term apparently coined by Myers) is a "middle region" of the subliminal self where a strange fabrication of inner romances perpetually goes on. Its great explorer was Flournoy with his research on Helen Smith and other mediums. In this conception the unconscious seems to be continually concerned with creating fictions and myths, which sometimes remain unconscious or appear only in dreams. Sometimes they take the form of daydreams that evolve spontaneously in the background of the subject's mind (a fact hinted at by Charcot). Sometimes, these functions are acted out in the form of somnambulism, hypnosis, possession, medium's trance, mythomania, or certain delusions. Sometimes the mythopoetic functions express themselves organically, and this suggests one of the possible concepts of hysteria. It is surprising, however, to see that the notion of the mythopoetic function of the unconscious, which seemed so promising, was not more fully investigated.
>
> (Ellenberger 1970, p.318)

It is hoped that the present work will help to redress this injustice, and show how important the mythopoetic function is, and how it can be an enrichment to the whole way in which we conceive of the normal personality, as Mary Watkins (1986) more than anyone else has shown.

The first psychologist I can find who dealt with the idea in a way which seems to throw off the historical distortions was William James. Hermans also finds in James an interesting precursor of his own approach. He started working on his great book *The Principles of Psychology* in about 1878, and it was published in 1890. In it he talked about social selves, and reckoned that people had many social selves, each of which could be called up in an appropriate situation.

> Starting with the discoveries of Richet and Taine, the unconscious became an active part of the personality as well as a reservoir of the emotions and of forgotten or repressed facts. Tarde, in particular, showed that the unconscious loses none of its dynamism and that the past experiences of a child may in some cases influence his actions in adult life. We have here a very different conception of the unconscious, one which is remarkably close to the Freudian concept.
>
> (Chertok & de Saussure 1979, p.168)

All through the 1890s Charcot and Janet and their colleagues were working on the problems of hysteria, and linking them with the phenomena of hypnosis. They talked about secondary personalities, dissociated from the primary personality, but saw this as something definitely in the area of the abnormal.

In 1892 the famous psychologist Binet published a book on alterations in personality in which he says:

> One observes that in a large number of people, placed in the most diverse conditions, the normal unity of consciousness is disintegrated. Several distinct consciousnesses arise, each of which may have perceptions, a memory, and even a moral character, of its own . . . Consequently, the limits of our personal and conscious memory are no more absolute limits than are those of our present consciousness. Beyond these lines there are memories, just as there are perceptions and reasoning processes, and what we know about ourselves is but a part, perhaps a very small part, of what we are.
>
> (Binet 1892, p.243)

Ribot published a book in 1895 which explicitly denied the existence of a superordinate self and postulated the existence of multiple selves.

In 1897 the great psychologist James M Baldwin published the first social psychology text, and in it gave some credence to the possibility of multiple selves, based on social conditioning.

In the field of philosophy, too, there was an interest at this time, and one of the most eloquent statements was made by the British Hegelian, William Wallace, when he said:

> We have hardly formed our resolve when we regret it: the voices of our other selves, of that manifold pack of half-formed personalities within us, none of which we dare honestly disown, are raised in protest against the usurping monarchy of our overt resolve.
>
> (Wallace 1898, p.109)

And so we come into the early years of the present century. In 1904 Sidis and Goodhart came out as saying the multiple personality was just an exaggerated expression of something which was actually quite normal in the human personality. Different selves are elicited by different situations.

H F Ellenberger (1970) draws attention to the upsurge during the early part of this century of a literature concerned with subtler descriptions of the many facets of human personality, and their interplay. He quotes in particular Marcel Proust, who maintained that the personality can be "composed of many little egos, distinct though side by side". Ellenberger feels that hypnotism provided the first model of the human mind as a double ego, and in discussing the multiple personality he recommends the notion that the personality is "like a matrix from which whole sets of sub-personalities could emerge and differentiate themselves". He discusses also the important question of what can happen once we give names to certain phenomena; I-positions may develop spontaneously, but they may also be influenced by suggestion, exaggerated by investigators and established more firmly through personification. Ellenberger quotes Janet's observation that "once baptized the unconscious personality is more clear and definite; it shows its psychological traits more clearly".

Similarly, Decker (1986) makes the point about Proust and others of this earlier time in history:

> These authors [Pirandello, Proust, Joyce, Woolf] share an interest in the unconscious in its many manifestations, no longer primarily emphasizing the obvious aspects of unconscious phenomena as seen in hypnotism and dual personality. They have left the stark dichotomies of awake vs. hypnotized, or personality A vs. personality B. They are dealing with multiplicity in personality rather than the flagrant multiple personality, yet with a recognition that illness and bizarreness can be present in the more muted manifestation. Proust, for instance, mentions only one clear-cut case of dual personality. He was interested instead in the many facets of personality in all of us. Personality changes from moment to moment, depending on place, time, and our companions. There is no one "real" ego, but rather a succession of egos, or the alternating dominance of different aspects of the ego. Virginia Woolf in *The Waves* (1931) has her character Bernard say: "I am not one person: I am many people."
>
> (p.35)

These literary pursuits were paralleled by work in psychology and psychiatry. Jung was talking about the complexes as early as 1908, and had much more to say about them from his experiments with word association. Freud was very interested in this work, but did not come up with his division into the it, the I and the over-I until the 1920s. I would describe the over-I (superego) as a complex, in Jungian terms, and as a typical I-position.

In 1936 Kurt Lewin published his book *Topological Psychology*, in which he described how regions of the personality could become relatively independent. He said:

> The degree of dynamical connectedness of the different parts of the person can be nearly equal within the whole region of the person, or certain regions can separate themselves to an especially high degree from the others and develop relatively independently. This can be observed in the normal person and it seems to be important for certain mental diseases.

This is a very important insight, but it was never followed up in psychology generally, in spite of the great respect in which Lewin was held.

In the 1940s Melanie Klein started talking about internal objects as being very important in the understanding of infantile fantasies. And this led on to the distinction which the object relations school developed between the real or true self, and the false self or selves. We shall be taking this very seriously later on.

Since then there has been a burgeoning quantity of different applications of this general idea, all of which are dealt with in detail in later pages. All we wanted to do here was to outline in a brief way the early steps in the process. It is very common in psychology to forget the pioneers and the origins of the ideas we take for granted today, and this is a great pity. Even Hermans, with all his amazing erudition, goes back no further than Bakhtin and Voloshinov, with a nod to William James.

Political implications

Not only is this a concept which is important for psychology and psycho-therapy: it is also one which is crucial for political theory. Many theories of politics, both conservative and radical, say that the person is conditioned early into conformity with society. The pressures of society are so great, they say, that the person is bludgeoned willy-nilly into being the kind of personality which a particular society needs. It is difficult, with all such theories, to see any place for radical social change.

But if there are I-positions, it may be the case that some of them are conditioned by society, and some are resistant to such conditioning; just as in a family three children may be conformists, and the fourth may be a rebel. The less conditioned, or differently conditioned, I-positions may lie beneath the surface waiting, as it were, for their chance; and when the situation changes, these other I-positions may come to the surface and take over. Freedman and Combs (1996), in their important text on narrative therapy, have a spirited account of how these ideas can become very political if they are taken seriously.

This would parallel the situation in biology where geneticists say that there are dominant genes and recessive genes. The dominant genes have their way in normal circumstances; but if the environment changes sub-stantially, the recessive genes may come into play and take their turn on stage. This is the concept of the understudy, the player who comes on in place of the main actor when that body goes sick or absent. We all have egos and we all have understudies – recessive parts of ourselves which are only awaiting a chance to have their way.

This means that in a social revolution people can change quite radically in quite a short space of time, adapting to the new circumstances and helping to create them. Without some such concept it is hard to account for the remarkable phenomena of change in emergencies, when a whole different side of people may come out. But with such a concept these things become much easier to understand.

A warning

There is one warning which should be given here, however, and that is that I do not believe that any of these ideas should be taken as taking away the responsibility of the social person.

There have been attempts to say that if the idea of I-positions holds water, then it could be said that if one I committed a crime, then another I could not be held responsible. This has actually been tried.

John Watkins is a hypnotherapist with a great interest in I-positions, which he calls ego states, and he has described his work in a chapter in Corsini (1981), as well as in an excellent book called *The Therapeutic Self* (1978a). He was often used as an expert in legal cases where there is a defence of diminished responsibility due to the presence of a "second personality" or something of that kind. In one paper (Watkins 1976) he goes into the Patty Hearst case; in another (Watkins 1978b) he goes into the case of "Patricia W"; and in a third (Watkins 1984) he deals with the case of the Los Angeles "Hillside Strangler'. In each case the defence lawyers tried to argue that the person in the dock was in effect not the person who committed the crime – even if they happened to share the same physical body. And in each case Watkins argued that there were in effect two different personalities involved, one guilty and one innocent; and the one in the dock was the innocent one. There would be no way of punishing the guilty one without by the same token and at the same time punishing the innocent one. But in each case the court refused to accept this argument. It would be wrong to diminish the responsibility of the social person who is visible to all, or the legal person who signs cheques, owns property, enters into contracts and so forth. In that sense the courts were right.

So the warning is – don't run away with the idea that the concept of I-positions can be used to diminish any of our human responsibility for all of our actions, no matter how partial or onesided or inadequate the impulse behind it may be.

The notion of multiplicity within the person can be continually rediscovered, even by therapists who have no such concept in their theoretical system. In this book we shall be examining many aspects of this matter. This book goes deeply into the psychotherapeutic use of the idea, and deals with all the practical advantages and difficulties involved in using it when helping people change. And it goes on to show how we can even use the notion of I-positions to examine the real self, the higher self, the soul and the spirit. It even describes how we can dialogue with the soul, or with God.

Chapter 3

The brave new world

Let us now just stop here to consider where we have got to. Instead of the old world of better and better definitions, we have now entered a world of no-definitions. There are some interesting connections we can make here. But first we need to note that we have now shaken off the shackles of reification.

No more reification

Reification is that process by which we take a theoretical concept and turn it into a real thing. Put at its most general, it is treating things of one type as if they were things of another. Treating an idea as a real thing is just one example of this. Every time we treat a theoretical construct such as a subpersonality as if it were a real thing we make a mistake. The theories we have been looking at in the first two chapters do not make this mistake. It is very important to be clear about reification.

For example, Kohut (1984, p.55) criticizes the reification inherent in Freud's tripartite model, and later the reification of the ego by Hartmann and the ego psychologists. They wrote as if there actually were such a thing as the ego, and therefore there could be no questioning of such a concept, and so no room for Kohut's idea of a self.

Reification is similar to Whitehead's notion of "misplaced concreteness" (Kelly 1998, p.125), which is the way in which we can take something as abstract as the schizoid position, and start to treat it as if it were a real thing. If someone said that there might be no such thing as a schizoid position, anyone who thought it was a real thing would be unable to hear that, or accept it. That would be falling into the trap of objectivism. There is a good discussion of objectivism and scientism in Mahoney (1992).

Talking about things, or ourselves and others as though we were things, keeps out any emotional responses or other genuine involvement, as Perls used to say. If we take something like depression as a real thing, rather than as a way of describing certain processes in certain contexts, we fall into the trap of objectivism, and what is sometimes called "the myth of the given" (Wilber 2000a, p.163).

Objectivism, like scientism, or positivism, assumes that there is a truth out there that is independent of anyone's subjective opinions. This is now a discredited view, and we now realize much better how truth is constructed in social contexts. We talk about *a* truth rather than *the* truth. Someone told me that in one of the psychosynthesis institutes they used a whiteboard which had printed in one corner "This is not the truth".

Putting all this together, we see that concepts such as the ego, the unconscious, the oral personality, the masochistic posture and so forth come in the realm of theory. They are concepts which may or may not be useful in certain contexts. They do not represent The Truth.

The drawback with the notion of subpersonalities is that it is all too easy to imagine that they really exist. And then questions arise such as: How many subpersonalities are there? Where do they come from? Does everyone have the same ones? Are they parts of the unconscious? And as we have seen, there have been attempts to say that it was the subpersonality that committed the crime. In other words, such a concept can lead to a festival of reification.

But with I-positions this is much less likely to happen. They are clearly not solid and fleshy: they come and go with the situation.

> In this conception *I* has the possibility to move, as in a space, from one position to the other in accordance with changes in situation and time. The *I* fluctuates among different and even opposed positions. The voices function like interacting characters in a story.
>
> (Hermans 2004, p.19)

It needs to be pointed out that we are now in the realm of social constructivism.

The varieties of social constructionism

The basic case of social constructivism, as described for example by Kenneth Gergen (1985), is that knowledge, scientific or otherwise, is not obtained by objective means but is constructed through social discourse. Hence the study of dialogue and discourse and text become extremely important. No single point of view is more valid than another, because all points of view are embedded in a social context which give them meaning. "Such a view does not obliterate empirical science; it simply removes its privilege of claiming truth beyond community" (Gergen 1997). However, within this general outlook there are a number of important differences.

The first step seems to be to outline the various approaches within this field, and to see what they are actually saying, and whether they are all saying the same thing. Scott Greer (1997) suggests that we should distinguish between constructionists and constructivists. The constructionists (like Kenneth Gergen and John Shotter) advocate a more anti-realist and anti-foundationalist position, while the constructivists (like Rom Harré, James Averill and Donald Polkinghorne) believe that while knowledge is to a large extent a social artefact, there is still a "reality" beneath, behind and between our discourse about it. Greer makes the point that Nietzsche was one of the first people to take up a social constructionist point of view:

> That the value of the world lies in our interpretation; . . . that every elevation of man brings with it the overcoming of narrower interpretations; that every strengthening and increase of power opens up new perspectives and means believing in new horizons – this idea permeates my writings. The world with which we are concerned is false, i.e., is not fact but fable and approximation on the basis of a meagre sum of observations; it is "in flux", as something in a state of becoming, as a falsehood always changing but never getting near the truth: for – there is no "truth".
>
> (Nietzsche 1967/1901, sec 616)

This is a radical and starkly stated position, which is strikingly similar to the current issues within the social constructionist critique.

Kurt Danziger (1997), on the other hand, makes a distinction between light constructionism and dark constructionism. Light constructionism says that "among those points of view which do not claim a monopoly on the path to the truth, which do not prejudge the nature of reality, tolerance must be the order of the day. A thousand flowers may bloom, provided none of them is of a type that threatens to take over the entire field, if left unchecked" (p.410). Dark constructionism (often referring to Foucault) says that discourse is embedded in relations of power. Talk and text are inseparable from manifestations of power. While light constructionists such as John Shotter emphasize the ongoing construction of meaning in present dialogue, dark constructionists emphasize the dependence of current patterns of interaction on rigid power structures established in the past and protected from change by countless institutionalized practices and textual conventions.

Art Warmoth (1997) says "The fact that power relations are an aspect of communication (social discourse) should not surprise humanistic psychologists, especially those familiar with Gregory Bateson's work. But we should be alert to tendencies to stereotype or rigidify categories such as class and gender structures." There is a delicate line to tread here, because the humanistic approach is like the constructionist approach in having a liberatory tendency: in this respect we are on the same side, so to speak, in relation to the forces of mechanistic thinking. And the feminist critique of gender certainties (e.g. Gergen & Davis 1997) is part of this effort for both parties.

Cor Baerveldt and Paul Voestermans (1996) make a distinction between weak social constructionism, which says that there can be such a thing as natural emotional responses (although they can become connected with a sense of self only within the context of a cultural system of beliefs and values), and strong social constructionism, which denies the relevance of physiological processes altogether. "From this perspective, the states and functions of the body become a cluster of cultural instead of natural, that is, biological constructions" (p.695). This is not positing physiology and culture as polar opposites: it is merely saying that physiology is not to be taken for granted as foundational.

Perhaps the most radical form of social constructionism is that put forward by Paul Stenner and Christopher Eccleston (1994), when they say that the more the distinction between the real and the discursive is examined, the more it becomes obvious that it is precisely the meaning something has for people and what it matters to anyone (both discursive questions) that constitute its reality. So their approach, which they call Textuality, sees the usual objects of psychological inquiry as so many texts which we read and discuss as opposed to fixed entities or essences which we strive to know.

> Another way of putting this is that Textuality serves to worry or trouble the commonly held dichotomy between subject and object or knower and known. For us, neither subject nor object is accorded the status of already existing fact or pre-given essence. Rather, both are viewed as *socially constructed*: as continually (re)produced in discursive (and other) practices in the course of social activities.
>
> (p.89)

This enables them to question in a radical way the importance and even the existence of such things as attitudes, emotions, memory, personality, prejudice and thought. "It is a deconstructive strategy which serves to dissolve the very 'thingness' of the entity by drawing attention to the discursive work necessary to constitute and uphold the impression of 'thinghood'" (p.94). This vision of contexts within contexts within contexts is a difficult one to get hold of, and these authors are careful to distinguish themselves from various misdescriptions and misunderstandings which have been imputed to such a position.

It does seem clear, however, that they are strong and dark constructionists in the senses described earlier.

> We encourage a social constructionism whereby people are viewed as readers and writers (written upon and read) within the Textuality of

culture. People (and this includes people who are psychologists or social scientists) actively construct (and are actively constructed by) versions of the "way things are", versions which are always-already enmeshed with the moral, political and ideological concerns of Being.

(p.96)

So in the end they settle not for a critical realism, but for a critical polytextualism.

It should not be assumed that this is all there is to be said about the importance of constructivism. As Raskin (2007) has pointed out, psychologists have been guilty of ignoring a whole variety of constructivist sources such as Ecker and Hulley 1996; Eron and Lund 1996; Fransella 2003; Guidano 1991; Hoyt 1994, 1996; Mahoney 2003; McNamee 1996; Neimeyer and Mahoney 1995; Neimeyer and Raskin 2000; Raskin and Bridges 2002, 2004; although current psychology is perhaps most guilty of ignoring George Kelly's (1955/1991a, 1955/1991b) personal construct psychology.

There is of course a danger in all this of paying insufficient attention to the ground on which the social constructionists themselves are standing. And in recent times they have started to question this themselves. A rather long quote from Kenneth Gergen, one of the classic pioneers of this approach, makes the point well:

> While constructionist critiques may often appear nihilistic, there is no means by which they themselves can be grounded or legitimated. They too fall victim to their own modes of critique; their accounts are inevitably freighted with ethical and ideological implications, forged within the conventions of writing, designed for rhetorical advantage, and their "objects of criticism" constructed in and for a particular community. The objects of their criticism are no less constructed than the traditional objects of research, nor do their moral claims rest on transcendental foundations.
>
> (Gergen 1997, p.739)

This seems an appropriately humble statement, and it shows us how the social constructionists are capable of taking their own medicine. This is the kind of reflexivity which humanistic writers have often championed.

The truth, as Hegel used to say, is the whole. It is only when we can say everything at once that we can say – "This is the truth!" But since we cannot say everything at once, we must agree with the constructivists and the discourse analysts and the Lacanians and so forth that we have no basis, we have no foundation.

What we also do not have, and what the constructivists do unfortunately still have, is a belief in the "either-or". They ignore the warning of Mary

Parker Follett (a closet Hegelian, see Graham 1995): "Never let yourself be bullied by an either-or." They ignore the magnificent words of Hegel himself:

> It is the fashion of youth to dash about in abstractions: but the man who has learnt to know life steers clear of the abstract "either-or" and keeps to the concrete.
>
> (Hegel 1892, p.146)

Constructivists have a bad habit of making an excellent case for the primacy of discourse, and then letting themselves down by denying the importance of realism. It is an immensely valuable exercise to see through the pretensions of foundationalists, and to emphasize the importance of sheer human discourse; it is not a valuable exercise to then say that that is all there is. If there were nothing but discourse there could be no foetal experience (Lake 1980), there could be no birth trauma (Grof 1979), there could be no memories of anything before language (Chamberlain 1998), there could be no poets creating new words and new languages, there could be no out-of-body experience (Grof 1992), no near-death experiences (Ring 1984), no mystical experiences going beyond language. The mad effort to redefine all these things as forms of discourse is reminiscent of paranoid thinking, which sees the same conspiracy everywhere.

The either-or is a madness. It is closely connected to the idea of being right, which is one of the most dangerous positions in the world, and one which the constructivists explicitly reject. If we maintain our dialectical thinking, we do not have to slip into this dangerous mode. We can hold to the "both-and".

The beauty of I-positions is that they are clearly postulated for the moment, as useful terms to be used in the process of therapy. There is no claim that they really exist, that they have an independent life – they are brought into being by the situation in which they appear. This is a brave new world, where we do not need anything other than the present moment.

In Buddhism, there is a great deal of interest in the concept of the *shunyata* – the void. The idea is that at the highest levels of consciousness all the distractions of everyday life disappear, and we are left with the clarity of emptiness. If this is the final reality, then we are obviously right to deny any separate being to the I-positions. For the first time we have a psychological concept or construct which will not get in the way of this final realization.

However, there is a question we must ask. If all this is true, how can we still make the distinction between I-Thou and I-It relationships? How can we believe in the possibility of an I-Thou relationship if there is no I and no Thou?

Saving the I-Thou

There seem to be at least four lines of thought which can lead in different ways to the resolution of this dilemma. The first of these, and the most obvious, is simply to put the "'I' and the "Thou" into quotes. Then we could say that the "I" is simply the way an I-position appears in certain contexts, and that humanistic discourse favours this way of talking. This would enable us to continue to use the terms with the approval of social constructionists. However, this usage might not be acceptable to many of those within humanistic psychology, because it is difficult to think of oneself as something in quotes.

The second position we could take up is to say that the "I" is real only in a particular context. If we participate in the humanistic psychology language community, we can very easily talk about the "I", because it makes sense in terms of other constructs like self-actualization, authenticity and autonomy, all of which form part of that field of discourse. We would not be claiming universal or exclusive validity for that field, but simply saying that it was as legitimate as any other. This would be taking very much the Wilber (1997) line that what we have is a series of nested truths, none of which can stand alone, each of which depends on others. We would be arguing that the "I" was a text in a context, and in that sense valid and meaningful.

A third line to take would be to say that the "I" is not a theoretical construct. In fact, as we can see quite easily in issue after issue of the *Journal of Humanistic Psychology*, no one has ever come up with a good theoretical description or empirical investigation of the "I". I have suggested that this is because the "I" is not a concept but an experience. When we have a breakthrough into what Ken Wilber (2000a) calls the Centaur stage of psychospiritual development, we have an experience which we in humanistic psychology have named as an experience of the "I" or the "I Am" (May 1983). While we are having that experience, which is usually for only a brief period at first, though it may well extend over time, we are authentic. We relate to others in an authentic way; we own our bodies in a new way; other people experience us as clear and direct and truthful. It is basically an ecstatic experience, and I believe it is a mystical experience, although on the foothills of mysticism, rather than on the great heights. After it, we are more likely to say that we *own* our experience in a new way.

Like all mystical experiences, it is ineffable. That is, it goes beyond the categories of our ordinary discourse. It can only be described in paradox, or in poetry. If we try to bring it down into everyday discourse, the language of the consensus trance, as it has been called, we can only distort and misrepresent it. From this second point of view, we would want to say that social constructionism in all its forms is firmly located at this lower level. It glories in reducing all forms of experience to some form of conversation. It relies totally on language (hence the emphasis on the text) and regards anything which cannot be put into language as not really existing at all. Just as the positivists (arch enemies of the constructionists) used to say that anything which could not be empirically tested was excluded from the field of science, and therefore beyond the pale, just so the constructionists say now that anything which cannot be part of a form of discourse is excluded from their consideration, and beyond the pale. So if mystical experiences cannot be forms of discourse, and if contacting the "I" is a mystical experience, the "I" is beyond the pale so far as they are concerned.

Of these three positions (we shall come to the fourth in a moment), it is the third which puts us in the greatest difficulty with academia. Academia mistrusts and hates anything which cannot be put in a book. Whether positivist or constructionist, academics continually try to put beyond the pale anything which is experiential. That is why psychotherapy courses have such a hard time persuading academics that such things as experiential training groups, personal therapy or supervision belong at all in their field. They are hard to assess, hard to describe, hard to evaluate. They are potentially messy and hard to control. And so we have the spectacle of academic courses in psychotherapy and counselling which include no practice at all. There are some of these now and I predict that there will be more in the future. In a group, in one's own therapy and even in super- vision one may have a breakthrough: one may have a mystical experience – even one which may change one's life. This is not controllable: and if there is one thing which academics are about it is control. It doesn't matter whether they are old nasty positivists or new shiny constructionists, they are all about control. Nietzsche would have laughed.

The fourth position we could take up is to say that behind and beneath the constructivist positions we have been looking at there is a more fundamental issue – that of dialectical thinking. The humanistic position is the Centaur position, and Centaur thinking is vision-logic, dialectical logic (Wilber 2000a; Rowan 2001). If we think dialectically, it is clear that we have all the time been saying something paradoxical. If we say that we believe in I-positions, and also believe in a real "I", this is a huge contradiction. Where is the truth?

The truth, as Hegel used to say, is the whole. As we have said before, it is only when we can say everything at once that we can say – "This is the truth!" But since we cannot say everything at once, we must agree with the constructivists and the discourse analysts and the Lacanians and so forth that we have no basis, we have no foundation. And so we come back to the *shunyata*. We come back to the mystical assertion that the final realization of the "I" is that there is no I. In the same way, there is no I-position either. They are both inadequate ways of saying what has to be said if we are to carry on doing therapy. However, this does not mean that there is no use in such concepts. They can be very useful so long as we do not give them an ontological status they do not deserve.

Part II

The dialogical self in therapy

Chapter 4

The use of multiplicity in therapy

It may have been Janet and Charcot and their hypnotic colleagues and contemporaries in the nineteenth century who first really outlined the idea of autonomous or semi-autonomous parts of the person, and in fact it may well be that their way of putting it reified the notion of such parts too much, and led us all astray. One of the most significant figures to put these ideas into action in psychotherapy was Freud.

Questioning the Freudian legacy

It has often been pointed out how dramatic is Freud's whole conception of psychodynamics. It is interesting to see exactly what Freud says about the superego. Freud (1938) says, in explaining the origin of the superego:

> A portion of the external world has, at least partially, been abandoned as an object and has instead, by identification, been taken into the ego and thus become an integral part of the internal world. This new psychical agency continues to carry on the functions which have hitherto been performed by people in the external world.
>
> (p.203)

In other words, we have taken inside us a voice from our external world, and internalized it. This is the process known in psychoanalysis as introjection, a term originated by Ferenczi (1909) to describe the way in which external people, together with the feelings associated with them, can become internal objects of fantasy. The purpose of introjection is to keep in contact with important people when separated from them.

However, it can be seen here how the reification is taking over, and the internal forces and tendencies are being turned into fully fledged characters. This is exactly the fault which the current work is designed to correct.

Why Jung needs a critical look

One of the great pioneers in this field was Jung. Some of his first work, in the first ten years of this century, was with association tests, where the experimenter says a word and the subject comes back with the first word which comes into his or her head. Through the use of this device, Jung became convinced that within the person there were semi-autonomous systems which he called at first the feeling-toned complexes. As Frey-Rohn (1974) says, Jung's interpretation of these findings was influenced by the work of Janet and Charcot and his French coworkers on the phenomena of "double consciousness" and "second existences" which they had discovered in their work on hysteria. We have already suggested that their influence was far too much aligned along the dimension of concrete characters rather than temporary I-positions. Jung came to believe that the split-off, unconscious complex formed a miniature self-contained psyche.

But Jung went further. And this is a strand of his work which has been taken up very much in recent years by followers such as James Hillman and Mary Watkins. Not only are complexes a result of problems (usually traumatic, in Jung's opinion) and a cause of problems (such as lack of control over one's daily actions), they can also be an important and healthy feature of the total person in themselves. In other words, the job of the psychotherapist is not just to get rid of complexes or tinker with complexes, but also to respect, and encourage the client to respect, those complexes.

This notion, that the complexes are good and to be taken seriously as necessary parts of human development and functioning, has been taken further by James Hillman. Hillman is a modern Jungian who has taken particularly seriously the whole question of the imaginal life – the deep life of the psyche beneath the surface. He sees this as "no longer single-centred but polycentric".

> We are no longer single beings in the image of a single God, but are always constituted of multiple parts: impish child, hero or heroine, supervising authority, asocial psychopath, and so on.
>
> (Hillman 1975)

If we take this as our basis, he says, we can then do all sorts of good work in psychotherapy. All we have to do is to allow and encourage these semi-autonomous parts to speak their minds, to interact with each other, to change, merge, separate, integrate and differentiate, to transform. And to do all this the first step is to personify the complex. It is as if we had to admit that the ego were not the whole story of who we might be at any given time, and that even the self were not the whole story. "For the ego is not the whole psyche, only one member of a commune."

Here we begin to find the positive connection between our current concept of I-positions and the old idea of subpersonalities. In both cases the secret is that in therapy we can personify such problems. Personification is the secret link between the old version and the new one.

Personifying, says Hillman, helps place subjective experiences "out there". It then becomes much easier to have relations with them. And it then becomes easier to own them, to own up to them. One of Jung's great interests was in ancient alchemy, seen as a way of talking about the psyche and its processes of transformation in symbolic form. And in alchemy there is a process called the *separatio*, where the different ingredients are set side by side. "Only separated things can unite", said the alchemists. And essential to this separation, says Hillman, is naming the internal persons, who often appear to us in dreams and visions.

> We sense these other persons and call them "roles" – mother, mistress, daughter, witch, crone, nurse, wife, child, nymph, innkeeper, slave, queen, whore, dancer, sibyl, muse. But can there be roles without persons to play them? To call them roles and games is itself a game by which Number One may deny the autonomy of these persons and keep them all under his control.
>
> (Hillman 1975, p.32)

The beauty of the theory of I-positions is that they do not in fact postulate a Number One. Nor do they imply any ability to control them. They are basically seen as temporary and contingent, not as permanent fixtures of any kind.

Another Jungian who, like Hillman, has paid attention to this matter, is Robert Johnson. But whereas Hillman says nothing about how to go about working with the personified entities, Johnson does. He warns us that:

> It is a mistake to jump to conclusions and to call your inner person anima or shadow or one of those terms if you are not really sure. For every dream-person who fits clearly within one of the archetypes, there are many others who don't: They are just persons in your dream. In that case, don't force them into a mould. Let them be who they are.
>
> (Johnson 1986, p.77)

He thinks it very important to name the persons who emerge. But we no longer regard this as important, other than as a temporary expedient. It can be seen how in the past the temptation to reify the inner characters was impossible to resist, because it was not realized how important it was to keep to and honour the fluidity, the flow.

Active imagination: A fresh look

So this activity is called in Jungian analysis the use of active imagination. It was in 1935 (*Collected Works Vol. 6*) that Jung first used the concept of "active imagination". In active imagination we fix upon a particular point, mood, picture or event, and then allow a fantasy to develop in which certain images become personified. Thereafter the images have a life of their own and develop according to their own logic.

A classic in this area came from Barbara Hannah, who actually worked with Jung, and then taught at the C G Jung Institute in Zurich. She says that this method enables conversations to take place with contents of the unconscious that appear personified. It does not matter how the image may come, but the essential thing is to hang on to it and not let it go until it has revealed its message through dialogue. She emphasizes over and over again the distinction between passive imagination, where we merely experience a scene as if looking at it on a screen, and active imagination, where we enter into an interactive discourse which goes back and forth between the personified image and ourselves. Barbara Hannah says one surprising thing – that she could never do anything along the lines of active imagination in this sense with someone else in the room – she would have to be quite private to do it. This idea is also put forward by Marie-Louise von Franz, in her introduction to the book:

> In contrast to the numerous existing techniques of passive imagination, active imagination is done alone, to which most people must overcome considerable resistance. It is a form of play, but a bloody serious one.
>
> (Hannah 1981, p.2)

This is, as it were, the original and traditional way of using active imagination, but because of its solitary nature, it does seem to be very hard and quite rare. But in recent years the technique of active imagination has been developed by people like Johnson. He goes a considerable way beyond the older tradition represented by Hannah, and says:

> A good way to connect to the inner parts of yourself is to think of each dream figure as an actual person living inside you. Think of each person in your dream as one of the autonomous personalities that coexist within your psyche and combine to make up your total self.
>
> (Johnson 1986, p.76)

This way of personifying the complexes and archetypes has its dangers. If we regard them as firm and fixed we are robbing ourselves of the possibilities of change, movement, splitting and joining – all those things which are very simple in the language of I-positions. But Johnson gives details about how to do the work:

> I am convinced that it is nearly impossible to produce anything in the imagination that is not an authentic representation of something in the unconscious. The whole function of the imagination is to draw up the material from the unconscious, clothe it in images, and transmit it to the conscious mind.
>
> (Johnson 1986, p.150)

We do not actually need the word "unconscious" in this context. There is no need to postulate an origin of this kind. We have to be genuinely open and listening. But this is sometimes not easy:

> If there is something in yourself that you see as a weakness, a defect, a terrible obstruction to a productive life, you nevertheless have to stop approaching that part of yourself as "the bad guy". For once, during Active Imagination, you must try to listen to that "inferior" being as though he or she were the voice of wisdom. If our depressions or weaknesses come to us in personified form, we need to honour those characteristics as part of the total self.
>
> (Johnson 1986, p.183)

Sometimes these I-positions may be very powerful, especially if they come as archetypal images from the collective unconscious. We may feel we are dealing with something which is more than human. But it will still make sense to treat it as if it were human, because this is really the only way in which we can begin to discover its meaning for us. We have to filter whatever comes through our own experience: there is no other way.

> Often your dream gives the person a name. If not, you can invent a name that seems to capture the person's character. Or you can use a descriptive name. If it is a masculine figure, it may be Brave Warrior, Wise Elder, Old Miser, Sneaky Crook, Juvenile Delinquent, Young Prince, Trickster, Tribal Brother. If this is a feminine figure you may find yourself calling her Wise Mother, Tyrant Mother, Earth Mother, Faithful Sister, My Lady Soul, Lady of the Sparkling Eyes. If she fits the mythical role, you may give her a mythical name: Helen, Iseult of the White Hands, Guinevere.
>
> (Johnson 1986, p.77)

Hillman seems particularly keen on the Greek gods and goddesses, and tries wherever possible to name the subpersonalities along these lines, and Bolen (1984) and McAdams (1985) do the same thing. The dangers of reification here are obvious, even though there are advantages in such a move, because the Greek pantheon is very rich and very familiar to most of us, and there is a lot of literature easily available around the subject. And some interesting ideas can come out of this approach, as for example:

> In ancient Greece it was understood that all the gods and goddesses should be worshipped. Although each person had particular favourites, none of the remaining deities could be ignored. The god or goddess whom you ignored became the one who turned against you and destroyed you, as Apollo destroyed Troy. It is also true in working with our consciousness: The energy pattern that we disown will turn against us.
>
> (Stone & Winkelman 1985, p.243)

This is a useful and important insight. There is still a danger, however, that we can become inflated or misled by this emphasis on gods and goddesses. I very seldom find, in my own work, that people spontaneously come up with gods and goddesses, so to impose this would be a kind of interpretation on the part of the therapist, which could enhance any narcissistic tendencies on the part of the client. It seems better to me to stick rather close to the client's own experience, and to let the client name the I-position as it appears. Where I have found the idea of a goddess to be useful is when encouraging women to see strong aspects of themselves as female rather than male, along the lines suggested by Jean Shinoda Bolen (1984), who suggests that Athena, for example, is very warlike and very intellectual but also totally female. So a warlike and intellectual woman client can be encouraged to see herself in this light, rather than as an imitation man, as the general culture of today would tend to suggest.

The word "spontaneous" is very important in all this. These I-positions are not things we invent or choose. Rather do we discover them and work with them as a result of following the normal process of psychotherapy, where we take current incidents and uncover the hidden meanings behind them. The phrase "configurations of existence" is important too: these are things which exist already, and have a right to exist. As Mary Watkins (1986) puts it so starkly:

> We would not judge a play or novel with one character as necessarily better or worse than another with several characters. So why should we impose this kind of ideal on the richness of our own thought?
>
> (Watkins 1986, p.106)

After all, in the literature on personality development (Loevinger 1976) it is generally recognized that complexity and the recognition of different sides of the personality side by side with one another is a sign of maturity, of high development. For us to see a person as all good or all bad is regarded as less mature than to see them as partly good and partly bad, and so on. Why not apply the same reasoning to ourselves?

What we have to guard against here is the view that this is somehow unhealthy, or leading away from the main task of psychotherapy. As Mary Watkins says:

> Imaginal dialogues are often looked at askance by clinicians. The suggestion that a person ought to entertain more characters, allow them greater autonomy, and enable characterizations to unfold which are more vivid and articulated might lead many to believe that we are encouraging hallucination, dissociation or fragmentation of the personality, a dangerous weakening of the ego – and perhaps even that we recommend becoming a "split personality".
>
> (Watkins 1986, p.131)

But in practice this is not so. I remember one working class woman client of mine who said in a puzzled voice – "What I can't understand is how I take myself apart into all these pieces in here, and yet when I go out I feel more whole!"

So this Jungian work is very rich, and has grown over a period of 50 years or so into something which is very sophisticated and well worked out. But more or less of the same vintage is another approach, which is not a million miles distant from it.

Psychosynthesis and its problems

One of the earliest people to have started really making use of the idea of self multiplicity in therapy and personal growth was Roberto Assagioli. He introduced his system of psychosynthesis, which in some ways follows Jung and in some ways goes further, in the years after 1910, and opened up his Institute in 1926. So it may have been at any time between then and the publication of his work in English starting in the 1960s that he began working with this idea. Nowadays, of course, psychosynthesis forms one of the main schools working with inner dialogues.

James Vargiu, an eminent American practitioner of psychosynthesis who had worked personally with Assagioli, wrote the first workbook on this. In introducing it, he says:

> There are in each of us a diversity of these semi-autonomous subper-sonalities, striving to express themselves . . . So one of the easiest and most basic ways to facilitate our growth is to get to know our sub-personalities . . . The Hag, The Mystic, The Materialist, The Idealist,

The Claw, The Pillar of Strength, The Sneak, The Religious Fanatic, The Sensitive Listener, The Crusader, The Doubter, The Grabbie, The Frightened Child, The Poisoner, The Struggler, The Tester, The Shining Light, The Bitch Goddess, The Great High Gluck, The Dummy, to name a few.

(Vargiu 1974, WB15)

It is clear that at this time he is still using the more reified version of the idea of multiplicity. But perhaps it was necessary to start here, just to get the idea on to the public stage. He does caution that it is a mistake to think that they all function at the same level, or that they are predictable in advance. One of the most important mistakes, says psychosynthesis, is to think, as Berne does, that there are just three ego states (with subdivisions) and that everything must be some version of these three.

He says that in working with inner voices of any kind it is often found useful to think in terms of a five-phase process. The first phase is simple recognition – the I-position has to emerge in some way. As we have seen, this may be through the emergence of a conflict within the person, or it may be through a dream or vision or guided fantasy, or it may be through splitting an existing position into two – however it comes, the therapist enables the client to realize that it is there.

Phase two is acceptance. All this means is that the client has to be willing to work with the I-position; it does not mean that at this stage the client has to like it. Or it may mean the acceptance of one by another. It may mean a moment of daring where the person takes what may seem the enormous risk of entering into and being the very thing he or she has most hated and feared for many years.

This makes possible the third phase, of coordination. This means the discovery and working through of the relationships between the different I-positions. If there are interpersonal difficulties between two or more of them some process of conflict resolution or accommodation or time sharing may need to be worked out. This again may sometimes take great daring, but if it is carried through, this process may bring about some valuable change.

This then leads on to the fourth phase, of integration. Here we go further with the process of resolving conflicts among the various positions and enabling the emergence of a way which now is harmonious rather than fragmented or disjunctive or negative.

The fifth phase is one of synthesis. This is the last phase of the harmonization process, and it leads to the discovery of the Transpersonal Self. Unfortunately the psychosynthesis people tend to think of this as the final truth of the person, whereas I am suggesting that it can better be regarded as just another I-position. This places unity at the end of the road. We shall see later on, as we have briefly already in our mention of people like James

Hillman and Mary Watkins, that we do not always have to strive for unity, but it is a strong value within psychosynthesis.

Vargiu then goes on to give a case vignette of a session with a woman who discovered within herself three characters – the Hag, the Doubter and the Idealist. The Hag comes across as being critical and twisted, the Doubter is afraid and mistrusting, and the Idealist has unrealistic ideals, refuses to accept her limitations, and her spirituality is pretentious and desperate. In the course of the session, another character appears, who is not so clear at first, a greater self, a higher self. This higher self looks at the others and sees them very clearly for what they are. The therapist then suggests that the Hag, the Doubter and the Idealist go for a climb up a mountain, watched by the higher self. When they reach the top of the mountain, the higher self sees them looking at each other and leaning in together and flowing into one. A new person is formed. The client says – "And she has a bearing that's not puffed up, or on an ego trip, but sure of herself, knowing who she is. She's very, very solid." The client then goes into this new character and becomes her. There is some further work in this session, and a good deal of consolidation and working through after the session, but that is the main gist of what happens. Obviously things do not always go as smoothly or easily as this, but it is a good example to show the basic movement which psychosynthesis aims at.

This is really moving into the transpersonal area, and psychosynthesis, with its recognition of the Transpersonal Self (sometimes called the Higher Self, sometimes just the Self with a capital S) is very capable of sustaining this move, as can easily be seen in the work of Molly Young Brown, who speaks very easily about the Wise Being we all have inside us. She also speaks about the Observer, and about the Superconscious. This brings her very much into the area we now call transpersonal coaching, where we often ask questions as Brown does, such as "What is my purpose?" (Brown 1993, p.69). And so long as we do not get caught in the notion that there is just one purpose, this is fine. All the time we have to look out for being caught up into the either-or.

Ferrucci (1982) also has a good discussion of the use of I-positions within psychosynthesis. He has many useful things to say, and good examples to offer.

It is interesting that in coaching Sir John Whitmore has urged the use of psychosynthesis, pushing the idea that coaching could be a much more transpersonal discipline (Whitmore 2002).

Some difficulties with psychodrama

Another candidate for first use of the idea of multiplicity in therapy is Jacob Moreno. He used the approach, very freely and individually. Blatner (1970) mentions the multiple double technique used in psychodrama, and refers to Zerka Moreno's paper, which came out in the journal *Group Psychotherapy* in 1959, and was later reprinted in the book edited by Greenberg (1974). In it she says:

> Multiple Double Technique
> The patient is on the stage with several doubles of himself. Each portrays part of the patient. One auxiliary ego acts as he is now, while the patient acts himself as he was when he was little, and as he was soon after his father's death, another auxiliary ego how he may be thirty years hence. The masks of the patient are simultaneously present and each acts in turn. With psychotic patients the multiple double technique has been usefully employed when the patient suffered from numerous delusions involving parts of the body; each of the auxiliary egos then represented a different organ, responding to the delusional stimuli produced by the patient.

Now most of Moreno's techniques were developed in the 1920s and 1930s, so it may well be that this method was used as far back as that.

What happens in psychodrama, of course, is that the protagonist (client, patient) takes all the roles sooner or later, and experiences each of these parts, from the inside, as that person. This is crucial to all that we have seen so far and all the other approaches to come. We have to get to know the I-positions from the inside, by playing them, and not only from the outside by observing or describing them. The more recent work in psychodrama is to be found in Holmes and Karp (1991) with its excellent chapter by Peter Pitzele on working with adolescents, Holmes, Karp and Watson (1994) which has a good discussion of sociometry and sociodynamics, Karp, Holmes and Tauvon (1998) which takes us through every stage of the working process, and Moreno, Blomkvist and Rützel (2000) with its moving discussion of sharing after psychodrama, and statements such as: "As for me, having experienced psychodrama for almost sixty years now, I have come to think of it as 'The Theatre of Mercy'. It is a place where love and acceptance of what we think of as the worst aspects of ourselves are found. We experience our common humanity and learn what it truly means to be human. We learn to transcend the past and reach for a more promising future" (p.xi).

In a way it is absurd to say so little about psychodrama, because in a way psychodrama has a better grasp of how to work in this way than anyone else, but because psychodramatists do not talk very much in terms of I-positions, and prefer to talk so much of the time about actual people, it is perhaps not so surprising in the end.

It is very interesting that recent forms of research in social science have begun to use psychodrama as part of the process of research itself. Hawkins (1988) describes how his research group used psychodrama to explore their own actions. First each researcher sets up a character to represent the part of their research they have most trouble with, and dialogue with that. Then each person steps back and looks at the dialogue from a third position outside that, thus turning the first protagonist into a second I-position. The new observer now starts to dialogue with the original researcher, now a researcher I-position. And finally the person steps back to become a transcendental ego, watching and observing the whole thing. This is very sophisticated work, and it is appropriate that it should come from one of the originating disciplines for this kind of work. One has to be careful, of course, not to regard the "transcendental ego" as anything more or other than another I-position. The temptation to reification is strong here as elsewhere.

The problems with Perls

We saw just now that psychodrama allows many aspects of a person to be represented and to have dialogues. But someone who laid all the stress on the internal conflicts rather than on the external conflicts was the inventor of Gestalt therapy, Fritz Perls. Perls made a general practice of having an empty chair beside him, in individual or group therapy, on which to place the various members of our internal world. This makes it easy for us to talk to them, and let them talk to us, or to each other. Something that often comes out is a topdog and an underdog:

> The topdog is righteous and authoritarian; he knows best. He is sometimes right, but always righteous . . . He manipulates with demands and threats of catastrophe . . . The underdog manipulates with being defensive, apologetic, wheedling, playing the crybaby, and so on . . . The underdog is the Mickey Mouse. The topdog is the Super Mouse . . . This is the basis for the famous self-torture game.
>
> (Perls 1969, p.18)

It is clear that the dangers of reification have not been avoided. It is all too easy on this reading to regard the topdog and the underdog as real beings with real existence. The topdog is of course very reminiscent of the Freudian superego, but Perls pointed out that Freud never said anything very much about the equally prevalent and problematic underdog. The self-torture game referred to here is simply the way in which we very often entertain "shoulds" which we do not really intend to honour. We carry them round with us, and every now and then they beat us over the head with the thought – "I still haven't written to my grandmother" – or whatever it may be. The reply is something like – "I will do it, but I haven't got time at the moment". In Perls' terms this is the topdog and underdog at work. This of course lays the major emphasis on conscious experience, but this view also has a place for earlier and unconscious formations of I-positions as carriers of unfinished business.

It is interesting that the Gestalt school lays all the stress on polarities as a form of conflict. They seem to see everything in pairs of opposites, rather in the manner of the Personal Construct school in their way, or the Jungian school in another. So there would very seldom be more than two chairs in operation. The fullest statement of this point of view seems to be in Zinker (1978). In more recent years, however, the Gestalt people have moved away from Perls, and been more interested in other aspects of the field (Yontef 1993).

So far we have talked mainly in terms of persons, whether male, female or mythological. Gestalt therapy is more flexible, however, in enabling us to give a voice to the most unlikely candidates. First of all, as in the psychodrama example given above, we can talk to, and talk back as, parts of our own bodies. This is not as odd as it may sound. Even a psychoanalyst like Harold Searles can say this:

> One category includes instances wherein a part of one's own body is, at an unconscious level, not a part of one's body image but is reacted to, instead, as being a separate person to whom one reacts with intense jealousy.
>
> (Searles 1986, p.105)

If there is a pain in some part of our body, we may talk to the pain, and talk back as the pain. Usually when this is done, it turns out that the pain, or the part of the body, was actually standing for an I-position which may be more or less important. The reasons why this is possible are spelt out in psychoanalytic terms by Faber (1977) in a paper which discusses in a very sophisticated way the whole question of altered states of consciousness in Castaneda's work:

> As for the body image, it is formed by the deposit of images and symbols of key external figures, internalized by stimuli from without, fusing with sensory perceptions from within . . . People treat their bodies and themselves much as they react to meaningful persons in their lives.
>
> (Mushatt 1975, p.93)

The conclusions are inescapable. The internalized object of infancy and childhood is internalized into our very organs, into our very senses. To truncate the tie to the internalized object is to liberate, or open, the sensorial apparatus, which is rooted in the body. Hence, to receive the world differently is to perceive the world differently, and to perceive the world differently is to experience the body not only in a new way but in a renewed way, a way that attests to the restoration of the individual to a sensorial capacity that is no longer expressive of the early internalization of the mother, that no longer belongs to the mother. One's body is, at last, one's own.

In this way I-positions are open to all the forms of distortion found in dream symbolism – condensation, displacement, censorship and so forth. By working with them and bringing out their ramifications, we can begin to understand and to transform them.

This does of course throw a whole different light on the body. It seems to us at first that the person must be single because the body is single. But if the body is itself multiple, that puts another complexion on things. Let us now look at a succinct and persuasive argument on this point:

> To proponents of singular self-identity nothing would seen simpler than the human body as clear and irrefutable evidence for locating the structure of subjectivity in persons alone: one self per body. Yet appearances can be deceiving even if, like the peels of an onion, appearances constitute the whole of so-called reality. The body is both complex and ambiguous. Even its apparently obvious unity was less than obvious to the early Greeks. Bruno Snell notes, "the early Greeks did not, either in their language or in the visual arts, grasp the body as a unit." Both the use of plurals to refer to the physical nature of the body as well as the crimped joints in the early vase paintings suggest that for the early Greeks, "the physical body of man was compre-hended, not as a unit but as an aggregate."
>
> (Ogilvy 1977, p.108)

The same author goes on to look at the findings of research into the brain and body, and concludes that they all go to show that there is a good basis in the actual way that the body is put together and held together to say that the body can be seen as multiple just as readily as it can be seen as single:

> Granted the limitations of biological metaphors – physiological pat-terns neither prove nor cause similar patterns in history – still the body provides living proof that pluralized, multicentered systems of order can function.
>
> (Ogilvy 1977, p.115)

This is a very helpful approach, which enables us to escape from the feeling that we are doing something strained or unnatural, or somehow unrelated to the body. I-positions can seem to be located in the body.

Fritz Perls, the originator of Gestalt therapy, was extremely flexible in the entities he was prepared to put on to the empty chair, including such things as: "your inhibitions"; phoniness; "your smirk"; "the old man you saw when you were five and a half"; "that memory"; "the dream you didn't have"; the mountain trail; the car number plate; the pillar in the station; the railway station; the water in the vessel; the statue in the lake; the rug on the floor; the two rooms talking to each other; "your left hand"; Fritz; all these things could be talked to and could talk back. And as they did so, they turned into I-positions – sometimes quite familiar I-positions and sometimes new and surprising I-positions. And as the dialogue progresses, something changes, something moves (Perls 1976).

One of the interesting things about Gestalt therapy is the way in which it at first depended upon Perls and then virtually disowned him. But the acknowledgement of the transpersonal seems to be coming back in the work of Hycner (1993) and others. In transactional analysis as well the same movement has taken place (Clarkson 1992).

Berne and over-simplicity

And so we come to transactional analysis, which itself has a number of relatives, all derived from the work of Paul Federn (1952), an old psycho-analyst. All these writers and therapists call I-positions ego states. As we develop greater complexity of living, our own personality separates into myriad functions, related to and isolated from each other, in thousands of ways. We divide our self into patterns of behaviour and experience, each of which is appropriate for various situations, and we thrust from activation and awareness reactions that would not be adaptive. Who wants to worry about a mathematics test at a party, or plan one's budget at a football game? We call these patterns of behaviour and experience "ego states", and they are normally a part of us all. Even as society must separate its merchants from its musicians, its teachers from its builders, etc., so also does the "society of self" within a single human divide itself into segments for the accomplishing of its various adjustive goals. Thus, ego-state theory holds that normal personalities are characterized by organizational patterns of behaviour and experience that have been partially dissociated from each other for purposes of adaptation and defence. The book by Watkins and Johnson (1982) goes into this at some length.

One of the most famous examples of this is, of course, the Eric Berne (1961, 1972) idea that we all have within us a Parent, an Adult and a Child, and that these can sometimes be in conflict with each other. He calls them ego states, but they answer in many ways to our description of I-positions. Faced with a cream bun, our Parent subpersonality may say "Put it back!", our Adult may say "Better not", and our Child may say "Go on, have it right now!" The conflicts may, of course, be much more serious than that, as we shall see later on.

Berne actually has a very good definition of an ego state, which brings out some important points:

An ego state may be described phenomenologically as a coherent system of feelings related to a given subject, and operationally as a set of coherent behaviour patterns; or pragmatically, as a system of feelings which motivates a related set of behaviour patterns . . . Repression of traumatic memories of conflicts is possible in many cases, according to Federn, only through repression of the whole pertinent ego state. Early ego states remain preserved in a latent stage, waiting to be re-cathected.

(Berne 1961, pp.17, 19)

Of course all the dangers of reification are here in full force. But Berne was quite acute in the way he would observe what actually happened. He saw that sometimes the I-position could switch in with great power. Berne later likened it to the way in which a bull stops in mid-arena when the scientist who implanted an electrode in its brain pulls a switch. He actually calls it "the electrode" because it can be so dramatic and sudden:

Many people know the instantaneous turn-off in the middle of sexual excitement, and have observed the smile which turns on and then instantaneously off as though someone in the smiler's head had pulled a switch . . . The electrode got its name from a patient named Norvil who sat very still and very tense during his group sessions, unless he was spoken to. Then he answered instantly with a string of careful cliches . . . after which he crunched up again. It soon became clear that it was a strict Father Parent in his head who controlled him with the "sit still" turn-off switch, and the "talk" button that turned him on.

(Berne 1972, pp.115–116)

Of course we are here in the presence of reification, but as long as we add "as if" the observation is good enough. In general the work of Clarkson (1992) puts us more on the right track here.

Is Shapiro too fixed?

At about the same time Stewart Shapiro was starting to work out his practice of using what he called subselves in therapy. In 1962 he contributed a paper entitled "A theory of ego pathology and ego therapy" to the *Journal of Psychology*, and followed that up in 1976 with a brief popular book called *The Selves Inside You*.

In my office are ten chairs, but they're not set up for group therapy; they're for individual work – one chair for each subself . . . Sometimes I'll use one or two chairs; occasionally three or four; once in a while, all ten.

(Shapiro 1976, pp.13–14)

He introduces a new idea which we have not met with before, though we shall meet it again in the work of Stone and Winkelman. He believes in deliberately creating an I-position called the Chairman of the Board, who will stand outside the rest of the subselves, and make decisions about how to handle them. But he makes it clear that it is no part of the job of this functionary to exclude or eliminate any of the characters:

> We do not "kick out of the house" any subself or part of the personality but rather understand and reintegrate its energy and functions back into the self organization. In subself therapy there are no outcasts and no prisons to lock up the deviants.
>
> (Shapiro 1976, pp.17–18)

Shapiro has his own version of the typology of subselves. This seems to be a regular temptation of people working in this field. We have just been looking at the way in which Eric Berne handles this. This can actually get very complex, even though at first it seems so simple, and even oversimple. For example, I have found from various sources the following kinds of Child ego state: the Adapted Child (Compliant Child), the Natural Child (Free Child), the Little Professor (Mischievous Gamey Little Professor and Creative Inventive Little Professor), Sleepy (a primitive, highly dependent part of the Child), Spooky (that part of the Child concerned with symbolizing), the Adapted Critical Child, the Disturbed Natural Child, the Vengeful Child and the Self-Protective Child.

Sometimes it is not realized just how intricate these models can get. Yet no one in this field seems to see the dangers of reification.

Unlike Berne, he does have a place for something outside the subselves, and here he comes very close to psychosynthesis, actually using the same disidentification exercise which Assagioli developed:

> For example, you may uncover various subpersonalities such as those of the person who found a Clown, a Gorilla or Caveman, a Child, an Earth Mother, and Father Time. The disidentification exercise in this case would be, "I have a Clown but I am not a Clown, I have a Gorilla, but I am not a Gorilla," etc. After going through all the subselves, the person would say (or think) "I am I, a center of pure consciousness."
>
> (Shapiro 1976, p.120)

He also has a place for the Higher or Transcendent Self. What I am suggesting in this book is that we do not see the "center of pure consciousness" or the Higher Self or the Transcendent Self as somehow above the battle, representing the Real Truth beyond all the illusions. What I am suggesting here is that we regard all these things as more I-positions, with a function of their own which is just as important as any of the others. We shall examine these possibilities in a later chapter.

Shorr adds flexibility

Perhaps the most flexible of all the approaches to I-positions comes from the psycho-imagination therapy of Joseph Shorr (1983). It is curious that he makes no mention of using different chairs in his work, and he seems to be able to do without all the apparatus the rest of us find so useful. He uses polarities, groups of three, groups of four, and obviously there is no limit to the imagination in his work. I find his approach a continual inspiration and in spite of his frequent superficiality he has a lot to offer in the understanding of how to work freely yet intensively with personification.

In the 1970s and 1980s, there was a great and important growth in the approaches using personification. This has involved extension of the older work, and also some quite different work.

John Watkins and new problems

Rather similar to the work of Berne and Shapiro, but taking off in an interesting direction, is the work of the ego-state school, led by John Watkins. These people are prepared to use hypnosis at times in their work, and see this as legitimate. Like the others, they see the person as a confederation of component segments. The relations between these segments are expressed through the operation of cathexis. Cathexis is an unfamiliar word to most of us, though it is common in psychoanalysis. It means investment – when we are attracted to someone or something, we put energy into getting close to that person or thing, being with that person or thing, getting hold of that person or thing and making him, her or it our own.

The theory of ego-states holds that dissociation is not an either/or, but it is rather a matter of degree. When large patterns of personality functioning are relatively withdrawn from "the me", and when they are not too highly energized, they form the underlying entities in normal people called "ego-states". They interact, influence, and emerge (become executive) for normal purposes of adaptation and defence. We behave and experience things differently at different times, but we sense a continuity in the feeling of sameness. Perhaps it makes more sense to assume, as did Federn (1952), that selfness is an energy, an ego energy. When a thought, emotion, motive, or other psychological element is invested with this energy, then it is experienced as "my" thought, "my" emotion, "my" motive, etc. But when the thought, emotion, or motivation is activated by a qualitatively different "not-self" energy, an "it" energy, then it is experienced as an object, as a "not-me", and existing in the world outside the boundaries of personhood. Watkins and Johnson (1982) have a good discussion of all these points, which fit very well with the new theory of I-positions. It is as if one of the people in our dream is often given the character of "me", and the other people and objects in the dream are treated as "not me". But this is a decision, and like all decisions it can be changed.

This approach does not seem to have the same emphasis on polarities as does the Gestalt school. They offer a much more general theory, and one which I find more persuasive. Thus, ego-state theory holds that normal personalities are characterized by organizational patterns of behaviour and experience that have been partially dissociated from each other for purposes of adaptation and defence.

> In a sense, each of us is a multiple personality. We exhibit one person-ality at home, another at the office, and another on vacation. But usually these various "sub-personalities" are governed by a generalized "Federal jurisdiction", even as the States of Montana and Idaho must submit to control from the United States government. We sense a continuity of selfness at all times.
>
> It is generally unrecognized that each of us is not a unity, but more like a confederation of component segments. Sometimes these parts cooperate and smooth the way of adaptation to the world. At other times they exhibit relative autonomy from each other and, through internal conflict, give us our anxieties, depressions, headaches, phobias, and other painful symptoms.
>
> (Watkins & Johnson 1982, pp.129–130)

This links in very easily with some of the other material we have already been noticing about I-positions. It is interesting that these people, working from quite different premises, come to the same conclusion about the undesirability of merging all the characters into one central self or ego. Fusion, or the merging of two or more personalities into a "oneness", is generally neither essential nor desirable except in special circumstances. The therapist is there to see fair play and make sure that all the voices in the dialogue are properly heard. The therapist should act like an internal diplomat, working out compromises and resolutions between the various personalities. Watkins and Johnson make some new points of their own, as for example when they discuss the difficulties which some clients offer when they threaten to take some extreme action:

> Underlying personalities and ego states, being "part-persons", do not have the ability to generalize and engage in abstract thinking. They frequently think concretely and illogically like a child. It is common for an underlying personality to plot the destruction or death of the person

while believing that it, itself, will survive. Suicide is thought as applying only to one of the other personalities, not one's self.

(Watkins & Johnson 1982, pp.138–141)

This is certainly a useful hint for something to watch out for very carefully. And it may be that working with I-positions even makes it easier to become aware of this kind of possibility.

Voice dialogue and its limitations

And this leads us on to what is perhaps the most ambitious and well worked out approach to personification yet devised. Hal Stone and Sidra Winkelman (now Sidra Stone), who come from a Jungian background, have now broken away to found their own school. They have a lot more to say than any of the others as to all the ins and outs of actually working with I-positions, which they used to call "energy patterns". They justify this nomenclature by saying that this term more clearly points to the dramatic animating qualities of these selves, as they enliven us, causing us to think, feel and act in a variety of ways.

Stone and Winkelman use empty chairs or cushions in their work, and encourage the person to come to terms with the I-position in question. They encourage an Aware Ego to take responsibility for the dance of the sub-personalities. This means that the voices are always taken as in process, as energy patterns, as I-positions, in spite of the seeming solidity of the usual labels.

After the facilitator has finished working with whichever Voices have been facilitated during a session, the subject moves the chair back to the original Ego place and is asked to stand behind the chair. This is the position of the Awareness level . . .

After this, the subject is invited to sit down and resume the position of the Aware Ego. Reactions to the work and possible differences of perception between the facilitator and the subject are then discussed. The session is reviewed briefly again and is then ended with the subject in the Aware Ego.

(Stone & Winkelman 1985, p.55)

This is quite clearly a rather formal and almost ritualistic performance, and it seems to be quite a feature of their work. It is perhaps this use of the Aware Ego that is the most limiting feature, because they insist on coming back to the Aware Ego all the time as a necessary central reference point. I think at times it is unwise to insist on this, as it seems to perpetrate all the errors of ego psychotherapy, which ignores the unconscious, or tries to reduce it to insignificance. My own view is that dialogical self theory is much better from this point of view. The whole idea of an Aware Ego who is somehow above the battle, not involved with the others, seems questionable in the light of our new thinking – to me the Aware Ego is just another I-position, useful but not special.

The language used by Stone and Winkelman enables them to make another interesting point, which seems to me to tie in with ideas earlier associated with the name of Wilhelm Reich:

> In many individuals today who have been involved in the consciousness process, we have a new phenomenon. In their pursuit of freedom they have disowned their Protector/Controllers. They have struggled for years to become free emotionally and sexually. They meditate, visualize and expand in all kinds of directions . . . This rejection of the Protector/ Controller energy is amazingly common in parts of the world where people have been involved in consciousness work for extended periods of time. Conversely, in those parts of the world where psychological work is relatively new, the Protector/Controllers are very strong.
>
> (Stone & Winkelman 1985, p.94)

This may remind us of Reich's distinction between sexual freedom, where we have genuinely integrated our conflicts and got rid of our character armour, and sexual sophistication, where we resolve consciously to be free. The latter, he says, actually involves the inhibition of inhibition, and is even more tortuous and neurotic than the original sexual repression. To disown one's Protector/Controller seems very much to fall into the same trap. It is, however, possible to ask it to stand aside sometimes, so as not to get in the way. Genpo Roshi also makes this point.

These authors also handle in an interesting way the problem of the vulnerable child, which has come to our notice so acutely through the work of Alice Miller. It may be remembered that one of her most telling points is that the abuse of a young child may be actually repeated in the therapy room, the therapist taking up the role of the abusing parent. On this our authors say:

> The Children of our inner world know how to "be". Most of the rest of our personality knows how to "do" and how to "act". The gift to the facilitator in working with these patterns is that he must learn how to "be" with them; otherwise they cannot emerge. When dealing with the Inner Child, the dictum is: "There's nowhere to go and there's nothing to do."
>
> (Stone & Winkelman 1985, p.145)

This seems a wise and deep thing to say, and if therapists could take this more seriously they could perhaps avoid the pitfalls which Alice Miller more than anyone else has pointed out.

They also seem to be on the side of the angels, so to speak, in relation to the question of power. One of the perennial questions which therapists get asked is – "If you are encouraging people to be more powerful in their lives, and to take charge, as you put it, of their lives, is this not going to make them more oppressive and more arrogant?" After quoting a number of concrete cases, our authors have an interesting answer to this:

> We see again in these examples the basic difference between being powerful and being empowered. Being and acting powerful means that we are identified with the energy patterns on the Power side. Empowerment means that we have an Aware Ego that can honor, and to some extent embrace, both Power and, ironically enough, Vulnerability. Empowerment is certainly one of the inevitable outcomes of this whole process we are describing.
>
> (Stone & Winkelman 1985, p.164)

So a combination of strength and vulnerability, to some people exact opposites, seems to be a good way of looking at empowerment. And once we have seen it in this way, we can appreciate how particularly relevant this concept is to women:

> In a way, women are more likely to reach for empowerment than men. They still do not have access to traditional power and are forced to move ahead from an empowered position (power plus vulnerability) rather than a power position (one identified with archetypal parental energies) because in many areas access to the power of the collective is denied them. Because of this, many women do not develop the same kinds of Heavyweight subpersonalities as men.
>
> (Stone & Winkelman 1985, p.220)

This again is a question hardly touched on by other writers in this field, who often seem to assume that women are going to have just the same types of I-positions as men. But this is not necessarily the case at all, and it is good to be reminded of this.

There is in fact in the work of Stone and Winkelman a good appreciation of the special problems of being a woman in the patriarchal society of today. They talk a good deal about the types of I-position which it would be most useful for women to cultivate and make familiar. One of these is the Warrior. Not the kind of warrior which may spring to mind with a spear and shield, stamping and grimacing, but the kind of warrior we have become acquainted with through the work of Carlos Castaneda, Hyemenyosts Storm, Dan Millman and others:

> The Warrior energy has been unavailable to women until recently. It was considered unfeminine, castrating, or worse yet, some form of devilish possession. One can see clearly, however, how necessary it is for self-protection and how powerless a woman can be if this energy is disowned . . . The Killer Who Protects . . . Warrior energy is needed by all humans, both men and women, for self-protection. Needless to say, women are seen as life-givers and healers, and the thought that they might have any destructive energies spreads panic among the population . . . To be denied access to the destructiveness in oneself is to be denied another major power source. Sadly enough, it also causes all of the destruction to be projected onto men . . . It is interesting to note that this voice has been so thoroughly repressed in women that it rarely assumes the form of a female. . . It is far more likely to be a jungle cat, a graceful feline killer.
>
> (Stone & Winkelman 1985, pp.218–222)

So we have here a good awareness of the way in which we are living in a particular historical epoch, in a particular part of the world, with a particular subculture. They are telling us that we have to take into account the social context within which all therapy is done.

Since the original work of the Stones there has been a good deal of work in voice dialogue by others as well. For example, Miriam Dyak (1999) has produced a large facilitator's handbook, which includes a marvellous picture of the psychological world ("Personia") which can be used with clients.

Dennis Genpo Merzel (2003) has used voice dialogue thinking to devise workshops which introduce people to mystical experiences. These are only glimpses, but as genuine glimpses they can be quite inspiring and confirm people in their psychospiritual development. Sometimes known as Genpo Roshi, this teacher has suggested that there is here a new development in Buddhism.

Mahrer breaks the mould

Someone else who is well worth looking at here is Alvin Mahrer, a very interesting academic working at the University of Ottawa. He presents a whole humanistic psychodynamics, based upon the notion of I-positions, which he calls potentials – operating potentials if they are consciously available, deeper potentials if they are unconscious.

> Each potential constitutes its own zone of experiencing, more or less distinct and independent of the other potentials. It is as if each potential is its own mini-world of experiencing. In this sense, we are indeed multiple selves, multiple consciousnesses, even multiple personalities. Each potential is its own center, its own self system, its own personality.
>
> (Mahrer 1978, p.29)

However, although he does not use the language of I-positions, he clearly sees the potentials as in process rather than as fixed. Human problems, he then contends, mainly arise from bad relationships between the potentials. It is these conflicts and maladjustments which cause all the bad feelings, all the compulsive behaviour, which make us appear neurotic.

> When potentials are disintegrated, their relationships are fractionated, abrasive, disjunctive, opposed, disorganized. Instead of accepting and loving one another, they fear and hate each other . . . the nature of the relationships among potentials is the major determinant of problems . . . our theory turns to the disintegrative relationship among potentials, not merely for "neurosis", but for the whole spectrum of human suffering.
>
> (Mahrer 1978, pp.27–28)

What the therapist has to do is to get in touch with the deeper potentials of the client, deeper potentials which the client may not know how to meet or to face. The therapist tunes in to the client, bodily and emotionally, so deeply that he or she can speak on behalf of the client's deeper potentials and encourage them to change.

> The radical proposition is that the therapist is thereby able to be the voice of the patient's deeper potential, to take on its identity.
>
> (Mahrer 1983, p.57)

At the point where the patient is now able to take on this revealed identity of his or her own deeper potential, which may have been defended against for years, a breakthrough comes and the deeper potential reveals its positive form. There can then be good, integrative relationships with other potentials. Energy is released, and the patient is able to be himself or herself more completely. This is the actualization of the potentials.

This is clearly a radical way of handling the question, but it gets more radical yet. The theory of development is also important here. Mahrer's theory of development is that the person starts before conception, in the primitive personality field set up by the prospective parents. The foetus grows within this primitive personality field, and the baby is born into it. Within this primitive personality field are all the potentials of the parents, and the relations between them. In Mahrer's theory:

> basic personality processes refer to material within the period from a few years prior to conception to several years following birth. Therefore, a deep, broad, and profound experiential psychotherapy will deal with material from that primitive period. It will go beyond the infant as the experiencing nexus, and into the experiencings of significant figures during this primitive period.
>
> (Mahrer 1986, pp.286–287)

So in this approach the client is not talking to empty chairs, but talking to the inner potential represented by the therapist. The therapist is no longer there, so to speak, but is now speaking for that inner potential, that I-position. When I have done this kind of work, I have sometimes felt that I knew the I-position better than the client did.

This work seems to me radically different from all the other approaches to I-positions, but quite compatible with them in most respects. Mahrer is a fascinating theorist, who has made many important contributions to the field.

Hypnotherapy – feast and famine

When I started to write on these subjects, I knew nothing about hypnotherapy. But the more I went into it, the more I found I had to go into hypnotherapy and find out more about it. And it turns out, as we saw earlier, that the whole of psychotherapy comes out of the tradition initiated by Mesmer, de Puységur, Liebault, Bernheim, Janet, Charcot and the rest. Let us just begin by going back to some of the details of that which have not been mentioned yet:

> The first magnetizers were immensely struck by the fact that, when they induced magnetic sleep in a person, a new life manifested itself of which the subject was unaware, and that a new and often more brilliant personality emerged with a continuous life of its own. The entire nineteenth century was preoccupied with the problem of the coexistence of these two minds and of their relationship to each other. Hence the concept of the "double-ego", or "dipsychism". From the beginning, ideas diverged as to whether that other, or hidden, mind was to be considered "closed" or "open". According to the first conception, the hidden mind is "closed" in the sense that it contains only things, which, at one time or other, went through the conscious mind, notably

forgotten memories or occasionally memories of impressions that the conscious mind had only fleetingly perceived, as well as memories of daydreams and fantasies. Some authors contended that this forgotten material could follow an autonomous development, independent of the conscious mind. The dipsychism theory was particularly developed by Dessoir, who wrote the once famous book *The Double Ego* (1890), in which he expounded the concept that the human mind normally consists of these two distinct layers, each of which has its own characteristics. Each of these two egos consist, in turn, of complex chains of associations. Dessoir called them *Oberbewusstsein* and *Unterbewusstsein*, "upper consciousness" and "under consciousness"; we get an inkling of the latter during dreams and clearer impressions during spontaneous somnambulism. Induced hypnosis is nothing but a calling forth of the secondary ego, which thus comes temporarily to the foreground. As for dual personality, Dessoir believed that the second personality had acquired such strength that it competed for predominance with the main personality. Everyone, he added, bears within himself the seeds of a dual personality. Subsequent authors supplemented that theory with rich material that included inspiration, mysticism, and mediumistic manifestations.

(Ellenberger 1970, pp.145–146)

It can be seen here how much of what we are saying in this book was anticipated years ago by the hypnotists. And they did not stop there. They went on to get nearer still to present-day ideas, going on from the idea of dual personality (dipsychism) to the idea of multiplicity in the personality, or polypsychism.

This word seems to have been coined by the magnetizer Durand (de Gros). He claimed that the human organism consisted of anatomical segments, each of which had a psychic ego of its own, and all of them subjected to a general ego, the Ego-in-Chief, which was our usual consciousness. In this legion each subego had a consciousness of its own, was able to perceive and to keep memories and to elaborate complex psychic operations. The sum total of these subegos constituted our unconscious life . . . The theory of polypsychism was taken up and given a philosophical elaboration by Colsenet, who linked it with Leibniz's concept of a hierarchy of monads.

(Ellenberger 1970, p.146)

Of course it hardly needs to be said how rampant the reification is here. Coming right up to today, and thinking about how these ideas need to be subjected to the most rigorous testing, it also turns out that some of the best and most accurate research on hidden personalities has been done in the hypnotic tradition, as Hilgard (1986) has demonstrated with a wealth of detail. He mentions that a whole issue of the *International Journal of Clinical and Experimental Hypnosis* was devoted to evidence and issues related to the kind of thing we are interested in here (April 1984, Vol. 32 No. 2). And it also turns out that much of the best current thinking about multiplicity comes from hypnotherapy. This was quite a disturbing finding, because I had always mistrusted hypnotherapy and thought that nothing very important could come from it.

The stunning book by Beahrs (1982) gives a practical and also a philosophical rationale for working with personification, and in it the author gives a great deal of information about other people in the hypnotic tradition who have made interesting and useful contributions in this area.

He has himself done a great deal of work with multiplicity, and agrees with others that:

> Our goal is not to be "rid" of a psychological process, but to shift it from the harmful or maladaptive ("pathological") dimension to where it is useful in its effect, so that what was once a symptom can truly become a skill.
>
> (p.82)

He takes the same position as we have seen to be useful many times before, that mood changes, altered states of consciousness, subpersonalities and multiple personality are points on a continuum of dissociation, with the boundaries becoming thicker and more marked as we go along that line. And he agrees with another of our positions:

> I consider dissociation to be essential for healthy functioning; in addition, I believe that it is a creative act. Kohut (1971) has taken the same position regarding vertical splitting, which I use almost synonymously with dissociation. Everyday examples of creative dissociating are dreams and fantasies, roles and specific skills, imaginary playmates, projection of both positive and negative aspects of the self on to others, selective amnesia for stimuli, and virtually any defence function. In each, an aspect of overall mental function is put in relief by dissociation in a way that enhances one's powers for action.
>
> (p.85)

> A single, gigantic, undifferentiated oneness cannot necessarily be considered a healthier condition than a complex cooperative whole comprised of many functioning subparts, like orchestra members, their power for action enhanced by division of labour.
>
> (p.113)

This is of course the emphasis we have already seen to be so important in the ideas of Hillman and Mary Watkins.

An interesting point he mentions about the use of multiplicity in treatment is that the therapist may not actually need to deal with each I-position in detail. He gives the example of a patient he had who was dealt with on the basis of just one I-position, which was worked with very thoroughly and a good outcome resulted. Later, this patient was able to report an awareness of five distinct I-positions, all dating back to childhood. "These had come together successfully without having been dealt with separately by the therapist" (p.104).

Another point comes from the work of Allison (Allison & Schwartz 1980), who classifies I-positions into three categories – persecutors, rescuers and internal self-helpers. The first two of these are relatively familiar, but the internal self-helpers not so. According to Allison, they have characteristics differing from pathological I-positions and are a great potential resource in treatment.

> In his view, they differ in having (1) no identifiable time and reason for their formation; (2) no defensive function; and (3) far more accuracy of perception, to the point of being "incapable of transference" and able to tell a therapist all his mistakes.
>
> (Beahrs 1982, p.109)

This is fascinating if true, and certainly something worth looking out for and exploring in more detail. It reminds me of the important idea of Langs (1982) that the unconscious of the patient is often very accurate about the unconscious of the therapist.

Karle and Boys (1987) have given an interesting example of one way in which early child abuse can be handled. This is of course just the kind of trauma which fits so well with the model given in an earlier chapter, and which has been found to be implicated in many cases of multiple personality. The client was a middle-aged woman who had been sexually abused by her father:

> She was asked to return in hypnosis to the time her father had molested her sexually, and simultaneously to observe the scene as her adult self. The scene was played out without the therapist intervening, up to the moment at which the child was ordered to her room. At this moment, the therapist asked the patient to enter the scene in her adult self, meet her child self on the stairs, pick her up, comfort and reassure her, and generally to act as she would to any child in such a situation. She was to continue in this fashion until the child was wholly reassured and at peace, and then to return to the present day. The patient reported successful performance of the task in terms of the child's restored

equanimity. Perhaps more important was the feeling that she could recognize in her adult self that her child self . . . was in fact innocent . . .

(pp.250–251)

Whether the client needed to be hypnotized to do this work is a moot point, and I personally would not take it for granted that this would be so. But certainly it is an approach which fits very well with the hypnotic tradition.

In general, work with I-positions is no more common in hypnotherapy than it is in other modalities. John and Helen Watkins are two people who have taken this approach a very long way. They make many of the same points that others have also made in this field, but add some interesting ideas such as the thought that working with ego states is like a kind of family therapy. This is, I feel, a very fruitful thought, and it seems worth while to look at the way they put it:

> Ego-state therapy is the utilization of family and group treatment techniques for the resolution of conflicts between the different ego states that constitute a "family of self" within a single individual.
>
> (Watkins & Watkins 1986, p.149)

They give the example of a student who could not study successfully. A strong ego state close to consciousness wanted him to study and was very upset when he could not do so. However, another ego state, identified as a four-year-old child, however, wanted more play and less study, and refused to let the student study unless he was treated better. The therapist made friends with the child, and persuaded him to play at night, thus permitting the student to study during the day.

> A week later Ed returned in great delight reporting that he had studied well during the past week and had gotten an A on his foreign language examination. He wondered, though, why he was having such vivid dreams and "in technicolor" every night.
>
> (Watkins & Watkins 1986, p.150)

It turned out that the child had kept his agreement and was playing at night. The student was not aware of this ego state until the therapist informed him about it afterwards.

So this is very interesting work, and I have acquired a new respect for at least some aspects of hypnotherapy since coming across it.

The ups and downs of Satir

A quite different and very original approach which comes from the field of family therapy was developed by the late Virginia Satir. She calls the subpersonalities "parts" of the person:

For one thing you probably have many parts that you have not yet discovered. All of these parts, whether you have owned them or not, are present in you. Becoming aware of them enables you to take charge of them rather than be enslaved by them. Each of your parts is a vital source of energy. Each has many uses, and can harmonize with many other parts in ways to add even more energy.

(Satir 1978, p.63)

So far so similar to other approaches we have seen so far. But what Satir then does is to use the idea to create a "parts party". She suggests that the focal person (who may be a patient, a client, a student, a trainee, a family member or whoever) uses imagination to bring up the faces (bodies, voices, movements) of famous people (fact or fiction, past, present or future, same sex or different) that have some meaning, positive or negative, for the individual. When at least six such people have been brought up, an adjective is put after each one, to sum up the particular reason why they came up – the particular meaning each one has for the focal person creating the list.

The next step is to imagine the people interacting. Satir's favourite way of doing this is to work with a group, and get the people in the group to take the various roles at the request of the focal person. But the same thing can be done with just one person, by getting them to imagine their people circulating round and round on a merry-go-round, getting to know each one more deeply as he or she comes round again. As this happens, each one becomes less and less the person they were to start with, and more and more the quality they represent for the focal person. As this goes on, the negative personalities or qualities very often seem to be more approachable and more manageable – "I cannot manage anything I do not own" – not so impossible as perhaps they were before.

There was a time when I thought I had to kill all those parts of me that gave me trouble. Now I see they may be my greatest helpers if I decide to make them my friends.

(Satir 1978, p.99)

Satir likens the person to a mobile, which only works well when all the various parts are balanced. We need in a way to stand outside the whole mobile in order to be able to balance it properly. And we cannot balance it properly if we pretend that some of the parts of the mobile are not there. Furthermore, there is a continual rebalancing of the mobile as it moves through different situations.

Satir has a deceptively simple way of putting these things. For example, when she comes to discuss anger and how to handle it, we get this:

> The child who throws a rock at his brother must be taught that such behaviour is unacceptable and that he needs to develop different methods for coping with his anger. Instead, he is often taught that it is bad to have angry feelings.
>
> (Satir & Baldwin 1983, p.232)

This is actually a profound point, but it sounds so simple and obvious that we may not recognize its profound simplicity. Similarly with the idea of the "parts party". It sounds at first quite banal, but in the hands of a fine therapist it can go very deep. There are actually four phases which can be considered: Meeting the parts (each part is personified and encountered as a person); Witnessing the conflicts between the parts (this can be brought out more vividly if there is a group, by asking each part to try to dominate the whole); Transforming the parts (through dialogue and negotiation until some stable balance is reached); and Integrating the parts, where the parts are again encountered, only now in their modified form, and symbolically accepted and unified. This is described in more detail in Satir and Baldwin (1983). The whole ethos here is to enable transformation to take place, so therefore there is no intention to make the parts permanent features, but rather to relativize them and help them to be more fluid, less rigid.

NLP and insane pragmatism

An approach which we need to say somewhat less about is that of Neuro-Linguistic Programming (NLP). NLP does not really believe in I-positions, but it does use all kinds of approximations to I-positions in its actual work. For example, in one of the NLP books it spends two pages on giving you a seven-step procedure for creating a part (their word, I assume taken from their work with Virginia Satir, for an I-position) and then they deny that there is any such thing as a part:

> The notion of parts is a good pace for most people's experience, but for me there is a bit too much anthropomorphism in the notion of parts.
>
> (Bandler & Grinder 1982, p.72)

To anthropomorphize sticks and stones may be dubious, and to anthropomorphize computers or robots may be dangerous, but to anthropomorphize people seems a perfectly proper thing to do, and may be about the only thing to do. In any case what we are talking about here is personification rather than anthropomorphization.

Possibly the reason for the lack of interest in subpersonalities in NLP is that they are so much influenced by the work of Milton Erickson, and he never did very much along these lines, so far as I have been able to discover.

However, some practitioners of NLP are more accommodating than Bandler and Grinder themselves. For example, Genie Laborde makes rather a nice point – that "inner conflicts are evidence of our potential flexibility" (Laborde 1987, p.187). She also has her own version of Satir's Parts Party: she invites eight parts to sit round a table, and appoints a Conflict Manager to facilitate the negotiation between them. This seems to be a solitary activity in her book. However, in a later book, she goes into more detail about multiplicity, regarding I-positions as resulting from the process of introjection. She points out that the incongruence we so often notice in people (the tone of voice not matching what is being said, or the gestures not fitting with what is being expressed verbally, etc.) can very often be traced back to conflicting I-positions within the person, some of them quite possibly unconscious. And she states very succinctly and well the main point of becoming aware of one's I-positions:

> By becoming aware of our internal conflicts, we can release the mental energy we have been using for repression, work out some internal negotiations, and use the released energy in our lives.
>
> (Laborde 1988, p.113)

What we then get, she says, is congruence – the cooperation of our various parts working in harmony, so that it is the whole person acting at once.

Another NLP person who has written about this is Lisa Wake (2007) who speaks of "parts" again, and links her view of this with many of the people we have already mentioned.

Sasportas tackles astrology

This kind of outcome is also found in another rather similar way of working, developed by Liz Greene and Howard Sasportas. They feel that the astrological chart, with its rather careful and specific delineation of influences upon the person and conflicts within the person, can be used to identify I-positions and suggest how they may be worked with. They say that the whole point of such work is not just to identify I-positions but also to disidentify from them and reconnect to the "I" that shifts from one to another.

Their outlook is rather Jungian, and Sasportas makes an interesting and novel suggestion that just as Jung says that each person (or Persona) has a Shadow (a negative or inferior part who embodies all the worst things we do not like or accept about ourselves) perhaps each of the I-positions has its own shadow. This is an interesting thought, and it does often happen that when one is working with one I-position, another voice will come through, and another I-position will advance and have to be recognized. Sometimes this may be a shadow aspect of the same one, and sometimes it may be describable in some other way. But certainly the idea of a shadow for each I-position is a thought worth playing with.

Another idea which Sasportas puts forward (which he says he acquired from the British psychosynthesis teacher Diana Whitmore) is that it is helpful to ask these three questions of each subpersonality:

What do you want?
What do you need?
What do you have to offer me?

As we shall see in the next chapter, these are very useful questions. Sasportas gives the example of an I-position who was a racing driver. He asked it – "What do you want?" – and it replied: "A flashy car." He comments about this that it is very gross, very specific and very exact. He then went on to ask – "What do you need?" The answer this time was: "I need recognition."

The need for recognition, he says, is more subtle than the gross want of a flashy car. It could be satisfied in a number of other ways, not just through having a car, and this may suggest other means of getting the same thing which are less expensive or more satisfying. The third question – "What do you have to offer me?" – brought the reply: "I have energy, drive and will-power to offer you." There is within the person a source of those qualities, and as long as it is defined as bad, and as just wanting flashy cars, those qualities will remain denied and untapped. This is good work in spite of the tendency towards reification.

Cognitive-behavioural therapy adds something

A complete contrast to this is the way in which the idea of I-positions is beginning to creep in to cognitive-behavioural therapy. This has come about because a good deal of research in cognitive psychology has now established the notion of self-schemas as being empirically testable and valid.

Two important writers are Hazel Markus and Paula Nurius, cognitive researchers at the University of Michigan. They talk in terms of selves and subselves, and introduce the very important notion of possible selves – projections of various aspects of ourselves into the future, an idea which turns out to have a great deal to say about the whole question of long-term motivation. They say this about therapy:

> Such thinking is, in fact, quite central to some recently developed therapeutic cognitive restructuring paradigms. The goal of such pro-grammes is to introduce alternative self-views into the individual's self-system and then attempt to modify the social environment so that these

alternative self-views can be more frequently activated to enhance their strength (e.g. Beck et al. 1979, McCullin & Giles 1985).

(Markus & Nurius 1987, p.164)

This view of therapy is very close to the general approach of what is now called cognitive-behavioural therapy, which is now well developed and advancing on all fronts. Later they published further research, again showing that these ideas are very much alive in today's world (Dunkel & Kerpelman 2006).

Donald Meichenbaum (one of the most eminent of those espousing the cognitive-behavioural position in psychotherapy) has made use of the idea of an internal dialogue. This is of course very appropriate for the general emphasis which he and this whole school places on self-statements – instructions to oneself, or selfputdowns, excuses and so forth. He says that internal dialogues are generated by cognitive structures which are "a system of concepts and judgements" (Meichenbaum 1977, p.21). It is precisely this sort of cognitive structure which constitutes an I-position.

Again in personal construct psychology, which Robert Neimeyer argues is part of the cognitive-behavioural approach, there is a concept of different levels of construction, such that whole subsystems can come into existence and be differentiated. The person can then slip from one to the other construct system, depending upon the situation. Neimeyer gives the example of a woman who was extremely efficient at work, and extremely inefficient at home.

As a consequence, therapy turned toward integrating these disparate subsystems, by importing into her personal life some of the organizational skills she used so effectively in business, and into her work some of the sharing of responsibility she accepted in other areas.

(Neimeyer 1986, p.238)

This sounds very similar to the kind of work which we have noticed elsewhere as appropriate to I-positions. The basic distinction which is so important is between detailed constructs on one level, and construct subsystems on the other.

Aaron Beck, who some would say invented cognitive therapy, has made a similar distinction between automatic thoughts and images on one level, and schemas on the other. He says that it is schemas derived from previous experience which are "used to classify, interpret, evaluate and assign meaning to that event" (Weishaar & Beck 1986, p.64). The notion of a mental schema (a whole subsystem within the personality), which is explained rather fully in another chapter, is congenial to the cognitive camp, and well founded within it.

In the same book, Richard Wessler, who has been particularly associated with the approach known as Rational-Emotive Therapy, argues that:

> Specific thoughts and statements may be seen as generated from schemata about oneself, the world and other people, and should be distinguished in therapy from specific cognitions. The relationship is not unlike that between surface structure and deeper underlying meaning. In a sense, every specific cognition may reflect underlying assumptions, which may be nonphenomenological. One important task of therapy, then, is to make clients more aware of their underlying nonphenomenological schemata. In other words (certain to be unacceptable to radical behaviourists), the task is to make the nonconscious conscious.
>
> (Wessler 1986, p.22)

This is obviously even closer to what we have been talking about elsewhere in this chapter.

Similarly, Goldfried (1982) has argued that schemas come at the level of therapeutic strategies, and that it is at this level that therapists of diverse orientations can speak a common language. So the language of schemas and I-positions may well be the language of the integration of psychotherapy.

Bogart comes to the bat

Another recent writer is Victor Bogart (2007), whose book contains one well worked-out example of how to work with I-positions, in Chapter 12. His name for them is personas at the moment, but this goes back to some much earlier work of his, and perhaps he could be persuaded to change now!

Biechonski and personification

Jure Biechonski in Estonia (2007a, 2007b) has actually produced DVDs showing how he uses personification in his work. He is clearly adept at this method, and uses it in a variety of interesting ways. It is a pity that he throws around terms like "Psycho-Neuro-Immunology" which seem a bit pretentious, and claims to be using hypnosis when he is sometimes not, but the actual work he does is very impressive and expert.

Hillman's critique

One of the most interesting questions to arise out of this account of how the idea of multiplicity is used by various people is raised by James Hillman.

We saw earlier that he is one of the main proponents of the idea that it is not only all right but very important to personify the mental entities which we have called I-positions. But then he seems to take away with one hand what he has offered with the other. He warns that "to take the archetype literally as personal is a personalistic fallacy". He warns against literalism and externality:

> We fall into externality all the time, even when internalizing in active imagination, taking the figures at face value, listening to their counsel literally, or simply by having to do active imagination at all in order to find depth, interiority, fantasy, and anima.
>
> (Hillman 1985, p.123)

And so he sees as a kind of religious neurosis the practice of talking with one's inner figures. He pours scorn on the idea of resolving the enigmas of life by means of internal dialogues with for example "my anima".

But this is very odd, in view of the commitment of Jung himself and many other Jungians to precisely the sort of practice which Hillman condemns. In the very same book, for example, from which the above extract is quoted, Hillman quotes Jung as saying:

> . . . start some dialogue with your anima . . . put a question or two to her: why she appears as Beatrice? why is she so big? why you are so small? why she nurses your wife and not yourself? . . . Treat her as a person, if you like as a patient or a goddess, but above all treat her as something that does exist.
>
> (Jung, 7 May 1947, letter to Mr O)

> [The patient] . . . is quite right to treat the anima as an autonomous personality and to address personal questions to her. I mean this as an actual technique . . . The art of it consists only in allowing our invisible partner to make herself heard . . . [O]ne should cultivate the art of conversing with oneself in the setting provided by an affect . . .
>
> (Jung, *Collected Works Vol. 7* §§322–323)

Hillman's thought seems to be that to treat anima in this way is to devalue her by reducing her to just one personality, whereas she is much greater than that. But on his own showing, anima is characterized by multiplicity, and we cannot relate to multiplicity other than by taking the many entities one at a time. For example, if the Great Goddess is Maid, Mother and Crone, it does no harm to relate to her as Crone only for a while. Perhaps later one will relate to her in one of her other aspects, and there is nothing about relating to the Crone which prevents one doing this. If I relate to my anima in the way in which she appears to me at the moment, that seems to me quite appropriate. At another time, she may appear quite otherwise.

This is clear in the work of Johnson (1986), and if we simply follow his hints we are unlikely to make the mistakes which Hillman seems to think so likely.

Integration of psychotherapies

What we have seen in this chapter is that a number of different theoretical systems are saying very similar and quite compatible things about I-positions. Could it not be true, therefore, that the concept of an I-position could help in the integration of the psychotherapies?

All evolution is a process of differentiation and integration, and we have seen in the past 30 years an enormous differentiation and proliferation of psychotherapies. The fat book edited by Herink (1980) contains details of more than 250 different therapies: of these approximately 34 per cent come from the 1970s, 36 per cent from the 1960s, 17 per cent from the 1950s, 6 per cent from the 1940s, 5 per cent from the 1930s, and 2 per cent from before 1930. This shows the remarkable increase over the 20 years from 1960 to 1980. If a similar book were produced today, my belief is that the growth would have slowed down considerably. Today we are in a period, I believe, of integration rather than differentiation.

And in this difficult period of integration, so much less glamorous and exciting than the hurly-burly of creation and innovation, we need concepts which can carry across disciplines and enable them to make sense to each other.

If we can say to the Jungians – cast off the shackles, and explore the world of the complexes with greater vigour and freedom; if we can say to the Gestaltists – take seriously the archetypes, and don't reduce everything to polarities; if we can say to the voice dialogue people – take your own ideas more seriously and admit that this can be a really deep and coherent form of therapy, stop being so nervous about always bringing everything back to the Aware Ego; if we can say to the Neuro-Linguistic Programmers – stop being so relentlessly trivial and adolescent and take I-positions and the dialogical self a lot more seriously as a realm with laws of its own which need to be respected; if we can say to the hypnotherapists – give up your insistence on speed and technique, and admit that therapy can take a long time, stop avoiding a real relationship with your clients; if we can say to Mahrer – drop your passion for polemic, and admit that you have a lot more in common with your colleagues than you usually make out; if we can say to the cognitive-behavioural people – give up this absurd notion that the cognitive can be isolated from everything else; then we shall be beginning to create a climate in which dialogue can take place.

The odd people out, as always, are the Freudians. Guardians of the treasure as they are, they are the least free of the therapeutic groups we have considered. They are trapped in the dogma of the transference and cannot seem to get out. Yet it would be so easy and so productive to allow their clients at least to have dialogues with their superegos. Actually, I am sure that some analysts have done so, and perhaps someone will write to me to tell me that this is all written up somewhere – maybe Ferenczi did it all in 1925 or something.

It seems clear from all the other therapies which exist that transference is not the only way in to the unconscious, not the only way to uncover the Oedipus complex, not the only way to uncover the Kleinian internal objects, not the only way to uncover the Kohutian selfobjects, not the only way to be thorough.

And in experimenting within the bounds of the theoretical framework, I-positions seem one extremely useful way to go. If we want to get the benefit of all the discoveries of the past 30 years, we have to take some risks. We have to try new things, and just because the idea of I-positions does not come from any one school, it perhaps does not bear on it the mark of Cain. I have come across no less than 27 different names for I-positions in the literature I have been examining, and this means that if there is safety in numbers, then the idea of I-positions is a safe one. But let us now look at some of the basic rules for using the idea of I-positions.

Chapter 5

How to

In the previous chapter we looked at a number of separate disciplines, and it may seem as though there is too much to remember. But as well as being terribly complex, this basic outloook is extremely simple. Let us now look at some of the hints and tips that emerge from all these years of effort. They enable us to distil, as it were, the essence of all this work, and establish the basic rules underlying it.

Rule 1: Spontaneity

When we elicit an I-position, no matter what the actual content, it must be brought into being in a spontaneous way. There must be nothing contrived or *voulu* about it. Then all we need to do is to carry on a dialogue with the image which has been produced spontaneously. Of course there is no one but oneself to play the other role, so it becomes a question of going back and forth between the two or more positions, just as we shall see shortly in so many other contexts.

> One can usually tell whether a person is doing real Active Imagination by the feeling responses that come out. If the normal human reaction to the situation in the imagination would be anger, fear, or intense joy, but none of these feelings are present, then I know the person is detached from the proceedings, just watching from a distance, not really participating, not taking it seriously.
>
> (Johnson 1986, p.182)

What we can see here is that the client is doing this in the presence of the therapist, and not alone as before. An important warning comes here, however. And this is a warning that applies to all uses of personification, whatever discipline it may be within, and whatever terminology may be used.

We must participate completely. There is, however, one line that should not be crossed. We must not stray from the zone of participation into the zone of control. In Active Imagination we cannot exert control over the inner persons or over what is happening. We have to let the imagination flow where it will, let the experience develop, without trying to determine in advance what is going to happen, what is going to be said, what is going to be done.

(Johnson 1986, p.182)

The point is that one must be willing to engage in real dialogue between the I-positions. It is not a question of what we would like to be the case, but of what actually is the case. The quotes here come from the Jungian camp, but they apply quite generally.

We always have to remember, of course, that technique is not what therapy is all about – it is the relationship that heals. One of the best writers on this is Rich Hycner, who says things like: "The therapist must incessantly struggle to bring his woundedness into play in the therapy, yet not make the healing of his own self the focus. In fact, it is this struggling that develops the self of the therapist" (Hycner 1993, p.15).

The basic case for the relational approach is made most fully and securely by Petruska Clarkson (1995, 2003) in her classic book on the therapeutic relationship, but it must also be recognized that there are also some deeper philosophical points that she misses. Wilber (2006) says there are three major meanings of "intersubjectivity". Intersubjectivity-1 is defined by isolated, atomistic subjects coming together through communication of signals; this is a type of Cartesian or mediated intersubjectivity. Intersubjectivity-2a is a coming together of subjects that mutually condition each other in the process; a type of immediate mutual apprehension. Subjective experiences arise in the space created by intersubjectivity. Intersubjectivity-2b assumes that the relationship between subjects is primary, and individual subjects co-emerge out of this prior relationship; a very strong, immediate, coming-into-being together. He has said that intersubjectivity is the field in which both subjects and objects arise. Both subjects and objects co-create, all the way up, all the way down.

These more sophisticated ideas are also compatible with the issues being raised in the present volume.

Rule 2: Beginner's mind

We need to have the right attitude towards the I-positions which emerge. Robert Johnson says that we should have a great humility here:

One must be willing to say: "Who are you? What do you have to say? I will listen to you. You may have the floor for this entire hour if you want; you may use any language you want. I am here to listen." This requires a formidable realignment of attitude for most of us. If there is something in yourself that you see as a weakness, a defect, a terrible obstruction to a productive life, you nevertheless have to stop approaching that part of yourself as "the bad guy". For once, during Active Imagination, you must try to listen to that "inferior" being as though he or she were the voice of wisdom. If our depressions or weaknesses come to us in personified form, we need to honour those characteristics as part of the total self.

(Johnson 1986, p.183)

I think, however, that Stone and Winkelman are right when they say that "Whatever energy we disown, life brings to us, exactly as we have disowned it." Each I-position is a distinct energy pattern. Each has a distinct facial expression, posture, tone of voice, and each creates a different set of energetic vibrations in its surroundings. It often makes sense to ask – "How old are you?" or "What do you look like?" – as we shall see in more detail later in this chapter.

But what kind of reality are we talking about here? Is all this something which is way outside anything practical or real? Someone who has written very well about this is another Jungian, Mary Watkins. She says this:

I shall place before you the view that imaginal dialogues do not merely reflect or distort reality, but create reality; that the real is not necessarily antithetical to the imaginal, but can be conceived of more broadly to include the imaginal; and that personifying is not an activity symptomatic of the primitivity of mind, but is expressive of its dramatic and poetic nature.

(Watkins 1986, p.58)

She goes along with the view of Franklin (1981), when he says that symbolizing does not merely reflect or communicate that which is already known, but is formulative, and creates meaning. So the activity we are engaging in when we have a dialogue between I-positions is a healthy and constructive one. Hillman (1975) defines personifying rather formally as "the spontaneous experiencing, envisioning and speaking of the configurations of existence as psychic presences". To call I-positions configurations of existence seems right. Some of the person-centred people are now talking and writing about configurations of self, which is a similar way of talking.

And there is a deeper point here which is worth making. It follows the suggestion of Andrew Samuels that *the arguments about the One and the Many in the psyche and the arguments about the One and the Many in relation to the schools of depth psychology are really the same argument*

(Samuels 1989, p.5). In other words, we are not only looking at multiplicity as a normal and valid way of looking at persons – we are also looking at multiplicity as a normal and valid way of looking at schools of psychotherapy. No longer do we look for the one great true school, to eliminate all the others and be crowned as King. We look upon schools of psychotherapy as contributors to the whole field in creative ways.

We saw earlier that Gestalt therapy focuses very much on polarities which naturally emerge in the process of psychotherapy, and that therefore there were seldom more than two chairs in use at any one time. One interesting exception to this is to be found in the work of Patrice Baumgartner. She says this:

> The patient gets stuck in relation to his existence or some aspect of it. He will not move with his feelings and so be a part of his own situation. Have him then see his existential situation outside of himself on the empty chair, expressing to it whatever he is aware of feeling. Sometimes when situational options occur, I like to bring in several chairs, imagining each alternative on a separate chair. The patient can simply let his various alternatives be, get involved with one of them, or explore his conflict by being with or becoming his available situations in turn. Several empty chairs are useful, too, sometimes for the patient's various roles. If he is stuck in one role, his others are then clearly available. Sometimes the patient will feel moved to get involved with another part of himself when he will do nothing with anyone else. Having these other roles "conspicuously" present helps. I do not remember that Fritz used empty chairs as vehicles for working through stuck points in just this way. The possibility occurred to me one day, and it has seemed to me to offer one more avenue of assistance. Sometimes people who come into the office weekly have special chairs which they designate for their various roles. They seem to use these physical places as emotional correlates especially if they feel stuck in one familiar role. I know something about where they are inside as I see where they sit.
>
> (Baumgartner & Perls 1975, pp.64–65)

This is one way of varying the two-chair method, quite dangerously open to the follies of reification. The way I like to vary this myself is to deliberately create another I-position myself, if the two polarities should get stuck. Sometimes this happens – the two protagonists get into a place where there seems to be nothing more happening. Then I may ask the person to get up and stand on a table or chair, and look at the scene from another position. At first I said (following Moreno's original suggestion) "Be God – what does God say about what is going on here, what does he say to each of those two?" But sometimes all I got when I did this was some kind of rather punitive superego, which was not what I wanted. So now I say – "Be a fair witness. You are an outside observer, who has seen a good many situations like this in the world. Tell them what you see going on, from your more objective position; give them any hints and tips you may think of value." This just helps to break up the logjam and enable something more to happen. It does not prevent us from going back to the first two characters and letting them continue afterwards. This witness is another I-position, which as we shall see later, may turn into some version of the soul. And sometimes we can refer to the soul directly, and say things like – "What does your soul say about this decision?" Often something very wise will emerge from this.

Again, we are not saying that technique is the answer to everything – it is the relationship which is at the centre of everything. Philip Lichtenberg (2000) has pointed out that the therapist can make sure that all four corners of the relationship are taken care of: For this to happen, both the I and the You have to pay attention to the "four corners" labelled A, B C and D: A. I am, I want, I desire, I feel. (Awareness of self.) B. I react in this way to you. (Awareness of self and other.) C. I want you to tell me what you want, desire, feel, who you are. (Awareness of other in communication.) D. I want you to tell me how you react to me. (Awareness of other in relation.) This is to take the relationship very seriously indeed, and in a later essay, Lichtenberg (2008) says:

> In every action in relationship, we are mobilizing our interior; we are connecting with various parts of ourselves, our many desires and wants, and we are acting to regulate the relationship we have. So there is a double directedness of every connection. When I talk to you, I am also among other things hearing myself, seeing my own process, watching you to see if you go to sleep what I'll feel like. So we are always doubly directed.
>
> (p.81)

He goes on to give an example of where he challenged a client of his along these lines:

> She wasn't looking at me; she was just talking in front of me. So after a period of time I said. "Do you know that I'm here? Would you tell that to me, and would you ask something of me in respect to what you've told me? How do you think I feel when you tell me that story?" I did a series of things like this; she was stunned. And it changed, dramatically, the whole relationship between us. Now she had to say, "This happened to me. What do you think of that? Or how do you feel when I tell you that?" And I could say, "Well, I really feel very sad when I hear you tell me that. And, is there something I could do when you tell me that that

would be OK for you?" And she said, "But you've already done it. You've heard me. You acknowledged . . . my loneliness."

(p.82)

This is to take the relationship very seriously indeed. And I myself have found it extremely valuable to take these relational steps.

Rule 3: Creative co-creation

Don't hesitate to be creative and embrace the impossible. We can always go back to a previous stage if need be. The utmost freedom is possible to attain if we simply go with what is.

The thing about questions deserves some further words here. There are certain questions which can be put to an I-position which have, over the years, become well established as useful. Those which I myself have found of greatest use are these:

1   *What do you look like?* It sometimes happens that the client has described this I-position already, so that we know what the client thinks it looks like, but what we are now asking is how it looks from its own position. Very often this is significantly different.
2   *How old are you?* This again may have been stated by the client, but now we are asking the character itself. And often this is a very revealing question, which can range from just a child to a very ancient being.
3   *What is your general approach to the world? If you had a motto or slogan that you lived by, what would that be?* This a very useful question, which brings out the basic attitude of the I-position, and may clarify things considerably.
4   *What is your main motive for being there? In other words, what are you doing for (name of client)?* This is often very revealing, showing what this character believes its task to be. Often it is very positive in appearance, but can be seen through. This can pave the way for a further examination at a later stage.
5   *What are the situations that bring you out? What are the situations where you think – "Aha! This is where I come in!"* This can be a very revealing question, and it often deserves some further probing at a later point.
6   *When did you first meet (name of client)?* This can often be useful, and can lead to some later probing, such as "What was going on in your life (or your family) at that time?"

All these questions are for I-positions which are elicited in the course of a session, and which have been mutually agreed between therapist and client. But sometimes an I-position arrives in some other way, from a dream or vision, and sometimes these more sudden and spontaneous characters can be quite menacing or otherwise threatening. Sometimes they can even take the form of a demon or dragon – a seemingly hostile archetype. For these characters, three questions have been suggested by the psychosynthesis people (e.g. Brown 2004) as we noted in the previous chapter:

What do you want?
What do you need?
What have you got to offer?

Instead of running away or squaring up to the threatening figure, as if we were afraid of it, we ask these questions in a calm way, because there is really no reason for fear. And when we get the answers back, they can be incredibly useful in suggesting ways to take this further.

Again, it is crucial not to imagine that technique is all there is. As Kahn (1991) tells us so succinctly – "The relationship *is* the therapy." This must always be remembered in all the detail and helpful hints. And it must always be remembered that the use of I-positions is very natural, often arising in the course of the therapeutic dialogue in an organic way, as Neimeyer (2009) shows in his book on constructivist psychotherapy.

Chapter 6

The new practice

Let us now proceed to the real meat of this book – the new work on the dialogical self and its companions. What we shall do here is to give examples of actual work done in the field, taken from research studies where the theory was used in practice. What we shall find is that

> Therapeutic conversation is the process through which the therapist and the client participate in the co-development of new meanings, new realities and new narratives. The therapist's role, expertise, and emphasis in this conversational process is to develop a free and open conversational space and to facilitate an emerging dialogical process in which "newness" can occur.
>
> (Goolishian & Anderson 1992, pp.13–14)

Let us look first of all at an early example, before all the recent stuff came up. This shows how the basic idea was present in many different places even at that early date.

An example

This example is given by Horowitz (1987) speaking of what he calls "role relationship models". The vignette he offers concerns a woman he names as Janice. In one state of mind she tried to feel and behave as if she were an active competent woman in a relationship with another active and competent person. Because this seemed to come easily to her, she and the therapist named this as the *tra-la-la* state. "The prototypical transaction was to be the expression of mutual interest" (p.56). Another frequent state of hers was named as the *hurt but working* state: in this state she "experienced herself as having developmental difficulties. She could ask for help and continue to work" (p.56), as long as she felt she had a teacher or rescuer to take care of her.

Horowitz gives an example from the third therapy hour. "She began in the *tra-la-la* state, with an animated and humorous imitation of what she planned to do." But then she slipped into the *hurt but working* state.

P: [Begins in *tra-la-la* style] Well, since last time, Doctor, [sniff] [dramatic play-acting] I, I find myself storing up things to tell you but, you know, things that happen or things that I think about a lot or something, so, tsk, hm [play-acting] I'll have to tell him this. [She pauses. The therapist listens quietly and intently. She becomes more nervous as she enters a *hurt but working* state.] I'm not sure why; whether I think you'll be interested, or whether I think it's relevant. Whether it's something I want to work out. There's something I'd like to work out; [pause, continues in *hurt but working* style] it happened, has been happening, guess it's still heavy [cough]. I got really, really depressed last week. I don't know what day it started and I couldn't really put a reason to it. You know, no incident, nothing happened. I wasn't thinking any train of thought and suddenly I just [pause] got depressed. And, uh [long pause] just [pause] it lasted for days and I would kind of – I was just sort of half functioning at work, hm, ttst, I can't think of a word, oozing my way through the day, and I managed to do a couple of wrong things and [sigh] I'm really upset about that.

(p.56)

The role relationship between learner and teacher was tolerable and somewhat desirable. But it was not easy to stabilize. She then slipped into a third state, characterized by what they called *acute self-disgust*. "The prototypical situation was the unresolved issue of her relationship with her mother. She felt self-disgust when she saw herself assuming her mother's identity, becoming a defective extension of her mother rather than a fully independent person" (p.57). Her solution to this was to switch back to the *tra-la-la* state rather than to remain with the impaired but learning self-images of the *hurt but working* state.

Horowitz goes on to say: "Obtaining supplies, even learning from someone, was dangerous in another way. Taking from someone could be seen as being too strong as well as too weak. To learn from another could mean to absorb too strongly and too much. She feared a state in which she would behave like a vampire and deplete the other person who gave too much" (p.57). This again pushed her into reverting to the *tra-la-la* state.

We can see here the way in which an I-position can shift from one state into another. What we do not see is any attempt on the part of the therapist to allow the different states to be fully personified and to talk to each other. But if we encouraged the *tra-la-la* I-position to talk to the *hurt but working* I-position, we might well find that the *acute self-disgust* I-position might not be needed at all. The use of personification might be extremely relevant to a case like this. We can only speculate.

Assimilation theory at work

William Stiles and his coworkers at Miami University (in Ohio) have suggested that therapy is a process by which one or more outcast voices become assimilated into the community of self. For example, one of their papers (Honos-Webb et al. 1999) includes a case study of "Jan", a 42-year-old white female. The form of therapy used was process-oriented psychotherapy, as described by Leslie Greenberg (2002) in Canada.

The researchers found that two main themes had emerged in the 16 sessions of the process: *superwoman* and *good-girl*. Each of these had a top-dog/underdog split: for the superwoman they were strength, endurance and independence versus feelings of dependency or weakness. For the good-girl they were approval seeking versus self-putdowns of various kinds. Jan also found it difficult to legitimate any of her own feelings.

At the beginning, Jan was unable to become aware of her neediness and weakness. Neither the superwoman nor the good-girl were able to recognize any such thing. But as therapy progressed, the neediness started to emerge and be recognized. At the same time the superwoman started to ease off and be more ready to let other people do things.

The good-girl became more and more aware that she was giving up a lot to gain the approval of other people. She became more and more able to give responsibility to other people to do various tasks, and less inclined to take everything on herself.

The authors say:

> We found it useful to construe this process as building meaning bridges between active internal voices representing the initially opposed experiences. Initially, for example, Jan's top-dog superwoman voice opposed and suppressed her emerging underdog voice of neediness and dependency. By the end of treatment, however, these voices could coexist and influence her behaviour flexibly.
>
> (Honos-Webb et al. 1999, p.457)

They go on to say: "The result of the assimilation of a previously unwanted voice into the self was not internal consistency but rather an increased differentiation and complexity" (ibid., p.458).

They argue that mature multivoicedness can be distinguished from pathological fragmentation by the fact that voices are integrated and engaged in dialogue with one another in a constructive way. And they end up by suggesting that the methodology for tracking voices could be extended to include more than two voices. This seems valid, in view of all the material in this chapter.

Here we have one of the crucial differences between the present approach and the previous schools we have considered. The idea of "mature multivoicedness" as something healthy and to be striven for is quite different from the old assumption that the final state must be unification. And this goes with the ability to conceive of the mind as a heterarchy rather than always as a hierarchy.

Greenberg and his group

The work of Leslie Greenberg has been mentioned. He and his coworkers have produced a number of books outlining the processes of what he now calls experiential psychotherapy. In his book, written with Laura Rice and Robert Elliott, from 1993, he makes it clear that he has been using personification for many years, going right back into the 1970s, and with serious research going on through the 1980s and 1990s.

> Facilitating the true opposition in the person's experience or identifying the core conflict is crucial, because if this is not done the dialogue will not develop and will become a confused intellectual exercise. Thus, the therapist works sensitively to refine the split until the true opposition occurring in the personality at the moment has been identified. The opposing sides are then put in contact with one another.
>
> (Greenberg et al. 1993, p.201)

One of the clearest examples comes from the paper he wrote with Robert Elliott (Ellliott & Greenberg 1997) using a two-chair approach. It goes like this:

> *Example of successful Two-Chair event.* The client in the following transcript (adapted from Greenberg 1984) is using two-chair work to address an unresolved internal conflict in the form of self-blame for a relationship break-up. In the transcript, speaking turns by the initially-critical self-aspect are designated "C" (for "Critic"), while speech by the experiential aspect is indicated by the "E." ("T" is the therapist.):

C1: You should have been able to . . . you should have been able to get through to him . . . when nobody else could, you could! You could have somehow . . . gotten him to see what he was doing . . . somehow . . . somehow communicated to him in a way that you could, you could see he was going down a path of . . .

T1: Tell her how she failed . . . you failed to get through to him.

C2: Yeah, you failed . . . you failed to get . . . to get through to him (voice breaking). You who, who knew him, who loved him, you . . . (crying) failed him . . .

T2: Say this again.

C3: You failed him. You didn't cause his breakdown – he did. But you failed somewhere up the road (sniff) . . . by not . . . not being able to just show him what was happening . . . but then . . . it was, it was . . .

T3: Change. Change.

E4: But I was buried in what was happening (voice breaking) (crying/ sigh) . . . and I was just about . . . having a breakdown myself. I had more than I could cope with (sniff) (sigh) . . . and even there . . . we'd be together, and I'd just explode in tears. I felt out of control. I felt like I was the one who was having the breakdown. And he was just angry.

T4: How do you feel when you say that?

E5: (sigh) I feel angry towards him (T: Right, right.) . . . for not being there for me.

The therapist then uses a brief Empty chair process, with the former lover in the other chair, in order to help the client to heighten and explore her newly emerging anger. After this, he redirects the client back to the two-chair dialogue:

T7: What do you want from that other part that says you failed him down the road?

E8: I want her to understand . . . I tried everything I could . . . I think she knows that . . . I'm not perfect. I can't be there for everybody . . .

T8: I couldn't.

E9: . . . I couldn't be there for (former lover). I was hardly there for me.

T9: Mhm. Try: You ask too much of me.

E10: You want too much . . .

T10: What happens?

C11: (Client changes chairs) I sort of feel softer, melting inside. I really do . . . expect too much.

T11: Mhm. Tell her this, I expect . . . I do expect too much.

C12: I do expect too much of you.

At this point, the Critic has begun to "soften" into compassion for the Experiencing self-aspect. The client then begins a process of negotiating between the two aspects. The episode ends 23 speaking turns later with the Experiencing self-aspect saying:

E24: And I, I want . . . I need you to trust me. I need you to . . . I need you in order to clearly know what I want . . . and to give me the strength to . . . the courage to simply be me. And I have got all the resources I need . . . except sometimes you . . .

T24: Mhm mhm. Change. What do you say?

C25: Um, I just sort of feel lighter.

(Elliott & Greenberg 1997, p.229)

It can be seen here how naturally and smoothly the interaction emerges.

This school, now known as the "experiential psychotherapy" school, makes the point that this approach is very suitable for dealing with the vexed question of shame. "The experience of shame is therefore a good implicit marker of an attributional split, and Two-Chair Dialogue is an excellent means of explicating this process of internalized shame" (Greenberg et al. 1993, p.191).

They also make the point that this way of working is important for handling Post-Traumatic Stress Disorder. "Two kinds of conflict split occur often in PTSD: First, self-blame for one's victimization is a form of self-evaluation split . . . and is readily worked with as a conflict split between a blaming, critical aspect of self and a guilty or shame-ridden aspect. Second, 'anxiety splits' involve a vulnerable self facing a 'coaching' or 'catastroph-ising' aspect of the self that dwells on fear-inducing situations" (Elliott et al. 1998, pp.263–264). This now seems to be a well established and well researched finding.

Pluralism and heterarchy

When we come to asking the question as to what the outcome is that is being aimed at in these studies, the most important point to be made is that the outcome is not necessarily hierarchical, with a big ego at the top of the heap. The most succinct account of the importance of heterarchy comes from the work of James Ogilvy. What he has to say is this:

Just as a free society requires a plurality of Somes, themselves each containing enough persons to support each individual in his resistance against the socializing Other, so each individual contains a plurality of selves who must in turn manifest yet another dimension of pluralization. Just as each statusphere is a Some in a social context, so each intrapersonal self must be a Some in the personal context . . .

Third realm rationality eschews the search for some basic level to which others may be reduced. Relieved of the quest for a lowest or highest level, relational thought can pursue the sense in which each dimension can alternate with other dimensions, in playing the role of pluralized content or determining context . . .

In short, a hierarchy is like an unambiguous pecking order. A heterarchy on the other hand has a structure like the game of paper, rock and scissors: paper covers rock, rock crushes scissors, but scissors cut paper. Scissors do not always lose. Instead they play a role analogous to what McCulloch (1945) calls a "diallel"; that is, a synaptic link that cuts across a hierarchical neural net (or "drome") to produce a heterarchical pattern of preference.

(Ogilvy 1977, p.113)

With this understanding, we can now see that a person can be integrated without falling into the error of the "monarchy" or "monotheism" which our authorities have warned us against. This is a most important point: to be integrated is not to lose or to play down or to be superior to the I-positions. To be integrated is to be more in touch with more of one's I-positions (some of which may have been transformed), particularly the ones which have been feared, hated and denied. And this enlarges the realm of our consciousness.

With the dilation of the domain of the operating potentials [I-positions now made conscious JR], I now am free to be anywhere in this expanded domain. This new freedom significantly expands the array of behaviors which can flow forth from me. I literally can be this potential or that other potential, and I can accomplish this switch with ease. In effect I am free to be each of these potential selves, and in each there is a distinctive set of behaviors. As a result, the total repertoire of behaviors which can flow forth from me is considerably increased.

(Mahrer 1978, p.504)

What we are talking about here is freedom, and the absence of compulsive fear. Instead of finding ourselves pushed around by our own processes, we are free to choose among them.

Becoming more integrated means that the center of the self is freer to move easily from one operating potential to another along channels of integrated relationships. Integrating persons enjoy their potentials far more than the rest of us.

(Mahrer 1978, p.505)

Again, we would now say I-positions rather than operating potentials, but this language of Mahrer is very well worked out and worth taking seriously. And this means that new possibilities are opened up. Things which before may have seemed quite out of the question now seem within our reach, and within our world.

What is even bolder and more audacious, the integrating person is willing to relate to deeper potentials [which] are not yet a part of the operating domain, not yet integrated into his sense of self . . . The weakness and uncertainty which are the deeper potentials can speak to him, can relate to him – and he listens. He is able to engage in a relationship with his deeper potentials, a relationship which enables him to engage in a more or less integrated fashion with potentials which are not yet fully integrated.

(Mahrer 1978, p.506)

It has to be said that the authors in the field of the dialogical self do not make this distinction between I-positions which are available on the surface, so to speak, and I-positions which are deeper and more hidden. I think this is a weakness, which would be quite easy to remedy.

If we want a much simpler version of the same points we can find them very succinctly stated in a little-known but first-rate book by Beahrs (1982), where he says:

*When is it useful or not useful to look upon an individual as a single unit, a "Cohesive Self"?
*When is it useful or not useful to look upon any one as being constituted of many parts, each with an identity of its own?
*When is it more useful to see ourselves as part of a greater whole?
I use the term "useful" rather than "true" since all are true – simultaneously and at all times.

(Beahrs 1982, pp.4–5)

What a succinct statement this is! As we saw earlier, the third point on this list, though less commonly stated than the other two, is equally important from a philosophical point of view. Not only Joachim, but many other philosophers have argued the case for this, from Hegel onwards. The British philosopher of the nineteenth century, Bosanquet, says this:

The true life is that of the whole, of which thought in the finite mind is a partial and incomplete revelation. The contrast of "pensiero pensante" and "pensiero pensate" precisely inverts the true relation. What really thinks is something more than any thinking act of ours.

(Quoted in Joachim 1948, p.101)

This may go further than we are willing to travel at the moment, and it is not essential to the idea of I-positions to agree with it, but it would be unfair to hold back on this. In the hands of Beahrs, such a view seems quite a sober statement of the obvious.

And it certainly agrees with the views of Stone and Winkelman, who as we have seen have done so much to illuminate all these questions by their painstaking practical work in the field:

From our perspective, all energy is part of the Universal Energy Source that may be referred to as God. When the voice in Siri's vision speaks to her, it is expressing the reality that belongs to any disowned energy pattern. Each kind of energy wishes to be claimed by us if it has been disowned. Each pattern returns to us in our dreams, in the personal reactions of our friends, in our meditations – each one of them is turning to us and saying – "Be still and know that I am God. Claim me, for I am that part of the Universal Energy Source that has been left unclaimed."

(Stone & Winkelman 1985, p.278)

We don't have to believe it in these terms, because the idea of I-positions makes a lot of sense even if we never push it to the limit in this way, but it is good to have the whole picture in front of us even if we ultimately decide to ignore part of it for the sake of utility.

In the next chapter we shall return to this transpersonal theme, but now it is time to look at another example of current practice.

The Italian work

This is taken from a paper by Giancarlo Dimaggio and his collaborators (Dimaggio et al. 2007). The protagonist was named as Katja. They say – "A dialogical relationship pattern contains at least: *a self position* (e.g. superior, looking for attention or disdainful), *an other position – including the therapist represented both by Katja and by his own words* (inferior, unwilling to grant attention, defiant) and *the type of relationship between them* (e.g., I am looking for consolation, other is busy with trivial matters and his or her attitude makes me angry). Each position in a story is treated as if it is a facet of the narrative developing during a session." We can see in the following extract from a session how the therapist can help the client identify the different I-positions within herself.

T: Last time we were talking about how you feel like a maggot, with a need for a protective shell.

K: What emerges at these moments is the opposite of the maggot, it's a hyena . . . The maggot is the most sensitive part of me, with more empathy towards other people. What's to the fore at present is the cynical, couldn't-care-less, standing-off side of me.

T: Let's play a game. Let's pretend there are three characters: the maggot, the character with the shell and a detached character. Let's find a name for the other two.

K: I'd call the little character with the shell the hyena and the detached one (pause) the lion . . . he's the king of the jungle and he reckons he's something special . . . he's detached in an arrogant way and is disdainful towards all the others.

T: Could you describe these three characters to me?

K: . . . The maggot's a kindly little creature, it's very kindly. And so it has to look out for itself because it's a bit like the poor little kitten, and so it hasn't got a shell and, when things happen to it, the consequences are immediate . . . when this happens and someone takes advantage of it . . . and it gets kicked in the teeth, then the maggot changes into a little hyena, which is very sarcastic and very calculating and lies in wait. It's aggressive, the opposite of the maggot, which is more accommodating and looks for a balanced solution. The hyena always knows where it's going.

T: The hyena is the one that appears on the scene when the maggot gets hurt.

K: . . . The hyena is very malicious. You need to be on the watch-out with it. But it's better than the lion, because it's aggressive and so there's an interaction with the exterior, which there isn't with the lion. When the lion comes on the scene, just forget it!

T: When does it come on the scene?

K: I don't know. Perhaps when the hyena gets bored, because it's not right even to be just aggressive. And so the lion turns up and stands off from this cruel world and lives in one where there is justice and injustice, and he's got total protection because he couldn't care less about anything . . . The lion's indifferent, his iciness is deadly and he's unapproachable.

It can be seen here how the daily interactions of the person are given more dramatic forms so as to make the work more effective.

Katja has little patience for getting involved in the struggle for self-integrity and the aggressive self gives way to the grandiose, detached and arrogant one, which stands off from relationships. It is to be noted that this is one of the few times that the grandiose character (Kohut 1971) appears clearly in this therapy.

It becomes clear that instead of the therapist contributing interpretations or insights, what is contributed is a way of looking at familiar problems in an unfamiliar way. The authors comment that this is like telling a story, even a fairy-tale, which enables the client to look at her problems in a new way.

In the above example, the therapist is active in suggesting new I-positions, and this is an important feature of all this work. It is often not enough to allow I-positions to emerge in a laissez-faire manner: the therapist has to use her or his intuition to tune in sufficiently to hit the right note.

It can be seen how complex these matters can become in the following extract:

> One voice feels "not up to it" and avoids having to do any tests or examinations. As a result, another voice emerges, which feels *guilty* vis-à-vis her parents, of whom she considers she is *taking advantage*. The result is depression. At the same time another voice feels *threatened and distrusts* the therapist, whom Rita sees as being an *ill-intentioned sadist* torturing her ("let her mind be tortured"). From another voice's perspective Rita feels *abused* like a *"guinea-pig"*.
>
> (Dimaggio et al. 2006, p.73)

This was work with a woman diagnosed as having a paranoid personality, which ultimately turned out well.

And now the Netherlands

The next example is taken from the work of Hubert Hermans and his ex-wife (Hermans, H J M & Hermans-Jansen, E 1995) and is more extended, showing how the I-position may change over time and must therefore not be reified or taken as more concrete than it really is.

> Mary, a 33-year-old woman, had bad memories of her father, who was an alcoholic. When Mary saw a man who was drunk or smelled of alcohol, she was overwhelmed by disgust and panic. In her adolescent years she joined the drug scene, which she also remembered with panic and disgust because she was sexually abused. She had great difficulty telling how she was forced to have sex, sometimes even under the threat of a weapon. As a reaction to these experiences, Mary "protected" herself by always wearing a tampon and bathing with great frequency. Her problems became acute when she married a man whom she loved very much. In strong contrast to her intimate feelings for her husband were the moments when she felt a strong disgust for him. Sometimes, often at unexpected moments, she felt a sudden fierce aggression toward him that was entirely beyond her control. When her husband was sleeping, she felt an almost uncontrollable urge to murder him. When he was sick and lying in bed, she felt hate and a complete lack of any compassion (it was, as she later realized, as if she were watching her father sleep off the effects of a binge). There were times when she felt like a witch, an alien experience that frightened her, particularly when the witch took almost total possession of her. She was scared to

death and sometimes felt as if she were being strangled by a power stronger than herself.

After discussion between the two therapists and the client herself, it was suggested that the feeling of being like a witch could be personified and turned into a separate I-position. It was felt that this might enable a repair to take place once the I-positions had been explored sufficiently.

It turned out that the witch had a number of defensive strategies: she could fly away from a threatening situation; she could change into something else; she could mask herself; and she could spit poison. The witch had then more resources than the more basic I-position that Mary usually occupied. In particular, she was better at distinguishing between safety zones and danger zones than Mary was: she was sharp.

The therapists then suggested two things she could try:

> First, she was advised to exercise (e.g., sports, biking, or walking) in order to expand her imaginal space and to express the dammed-up energy of the witch. Second, we proposed that she keep a diary in which she could write her daily observations, thus sharpening her perception. In the beginning of the validation/invalidation process, Mary primarily attended to what was happening . . . In particular, she trained herself to make fine discriminations between her own impulses, reactions, and emotions and those of the witch. It was certainly important for her to see at an early stage which situations the witch entered and took control of. To Mary's surprise, the witch appeared in situations that at first looked quite innocent, which explains why Mary often found out too late that she had gone too far in an emotional reaction.

Already, then, this distinction had proved valuable and insight-creating. The authors give an example of how this then resulted in a new ability to make valid choices in her life.

> A few days ago Fred was sick, with 104 degrees temperature in bed; he even had blisters on his lips. I made breakfast for him and brought it upstairs. When I entered the room and saw him lying in bed, I loathed him, and I thought, "Don't think that I'm staying at home for you!" (I was planning to leave for an overnight visit with friends in Amsterdam). Standing in front of the bed, I was thinking about this (with increasing venom) and became aware that the witch was coming up again. I left the tray with Fred and left the house for a walk. During this walk I felt that I could discharge a great deal of the energy of the witch. At the same time, I had the time to quietly reflect on the situation as it was: "He is sick, he needs me, and I want to care for him." I decided to buy a newspaper for him. When I came home, I

explained to him that I would stay the night at home and would go to Amsterdam the next morning. (So, I did not leave the decision up to him but proposed it myself.) Fred accepted this, and the next morning I went out to visit my friends.

This is very interesting, and shows how a new kind of control was making an appearance. Mary decided to take a break – a walk. During the walk, it was possible for the witch to weaken and for Mary to reassert her own identity. And this was done not by suppressing or abandoning the witch, but simply of being more aware of her presence.

A year later, Mary agreed to follow the same instructions as for the first investigation. That is, she first took her usual position as Mary and then the position of the witch. Indeed, although she seriously attempted to do this, she discovered that it was almost impossible for her to let the witch speak as she had done the year before.

This could only mean that Mary had now taken the lead in situations that were originally under the control of the witch. "In other words, Mary used the energy of the witch for her own purposes." It is important to understand that if, as I should have expected, the witch was put on an empty chair and dialogued with, that would not perpetuate or fix that I-position, but would simply make it easier to work with in the short term. The change process is not delayed but facilitated by such practices.

Hermans again

Let us now look at an example from Hermans in the Angus and McLeod handbook (Hermans 2004). It refers to a client named as Leo. He came into therapy with two problems: a negative evaluation from his superiors at work, and the loss of a loved partner, Laura. He became obsessed with this woman, and wrote an aggressive letter to her. He then started following her and her new lover around all day and phoning them with nightly telephone calls, to the point where she felt terrorized.

Leo was aware that he was increasingly behaving like a stalker, and this behaviour, in combination with the bad job evaluation, was his reason for contacting the psychotherapist.

This then led to further exploration where Leo identified another I-position which he named "the revenger". This character not only stalked the ex-lover, but also spent time and money visiting prostitutes. This showed that he did not need anyone to love at all. However, in the course of the therapy, visits to prostitutes disappeared, and Leo took up with a new girlfriend.

In going into all this more deeply, it began to appear that a third I-position had emerged.

> In discussing the relationships between the several parts of the repertoire, the therapist and Leo discovered that there was a highly influential background position: the dreamer. Leo explained that this position had been very important to his relationship with Laura, who always had been an ideal person for him.

The next phase brought the therapy to an end. He had already identified three different I-positions as "stalker", "revenger" and "dreamer". This client now identified two contrasting I-positions which he called "accepting" and "not accepting".

> For Leo, *acceptance* meant accepting that he was only as ordinary or exceptional as most other people in his environment and that he was not the unique reformer of the world. At the same time, Leo was invited to give more attention than before to the people in his environment and to accept their wishes, successes, and failures as realities.

In the process of the therapy, after having achieved these gains, Leo was confronted with an event that was quite dramatic: His new girlfriend broke off her relationship with him.

> This was, in fact, the ultimate test of his acceptance. Would he again become extremely aggressive, and would the revenger take precedence over all other positions? In the sessions following this event, Leo discussed the new situation with the therapist and succeeded in keeping himself under control. He and his girlfriend decided to continue their relationship as friends but not as lovers.

The theory behind this is well stated by Hermans (2002) when he says:

> On the interface between these traditions, Hermans and Kempen (1993) argued that the *I* has the possibility to move from one spatial position to another in accordance with changes in situation and time. The *I* fluctuates among different and even opposed positions, and has the capacity imaginatively to endow each position with a voice so that dialogical relations between positions can be established. The voices function like interacting characters in a story, involved in a process of question and answer, agreement and disagreement. Each of them has a story to tell about his or her own experiences from his or her own stance. As different voices, these characters exchange information

about their respective *Me's*, resulting in a complex, narratively structured self.

(pp.147–148)

Personification

There are plenty more examples we could look at, but what stands out is
that some of the current work does not use personification in any experiential way. In other words, the I-positions are identified but not allowed to
speak for themselves, or to each other, or with the client. This seems very
odd to me. What is the use of identifying I-positions if we do not allow
them to speak for themselves? The empty chair and two-chair techniques
are tailor-made for such possibilities, as Goldman has argued at length
(Goldman 2002). Occasionally this is done, as Leitner affirms:

> For example, let's return to Sarah, the woman who was sexually abused
> by her stepfather. Shortly after she presented, she began to refer to
> herself in the third person. It became clear that she experienced herself
> as a system of separated personalities, not all of whom were aware of
> one another. We often used an empty chair situation to facilitate
> awareness of the needs and issues of some of these personalities.
>
> (Leitner 2007, p.45)

Another example of actually working in this way is to be found in the
recent work of Robert Neimeyer at the University of Memphis, who
describes his work with "Mike" on his alcoholism. He remarks that several
methods come out of the basic thought of the dialogical self, including
externalizing problems in the narrative therapy manner, slow-motion
methods (Guidano 1995), Gestalt therapy, process-experiential therapy,
focusing and constructivist therapy (Neimeyer 2006, p.117).

In the next chapter we shall look at the way in which all these issues
become much more interesting in the traditions of group work.

Chapter 7

Group work and the dialogical self

Let us now look at the use of personification in group work.

The most common type of group to be found on training courses is the experiential training group, often called a personal growth or development group. Personal growth is a term coming from humanistic psychology (Rowan 2001). This approach includes person-centred therapy, Gestalt therapy, psychodrama, bioenergetics, focusing, experiential therapy, existential analysis and some of the feminist methods (Ernst & Goodison 1981). In this context, growth strictly means development in terms of the Maslow (1987) theory of a hierarchy of needs. This says that we all start off with physiological needs. When these are satisfied, we move on to safety needs, involving basic trust. When these are satisfied, we can move on to the higher levels as we grow up, for example learning our roles so as to be good conformists. As Kohlberg (1981) showed through his research, we can then continue growing, moving from the conventional to the postconventional forms of consciousness. Psychodynamic therapists used to avoid the term "personal growth" but in recent years many of them have adopted it. Of course they do not mean by it what Maslow meant, but something more like working through their issues: though of course Jung independently pursued the idea under the heading of Individuation. "The process of individuation is a circumambulation of the self as the centre of the personality which thereby becomes unified" (Samuels, Shorter & Plaut 1986, p.76). This means working through the hangups of the persona and the distractions of the Shadow and other archetypes. The paradox of working through multiplicity to gain unity is very common in Jungian thinking, and personification is very useful in working with archetypes and complexes.

Group work is particularly good for moving across what I have called "the Great Gap". This is the gap between levels 4 and 5 of Figure 1. This gap is between needing esteem from others, and looking to them to see how they expect us to behave, and moving on to giving esteem to ourselves and being open to discovering what each of us can be. Crossing the great gap begins when the group gives us a forum for questioning our customary assumptions and our usual roles. Being real is central in personal growth

Maslow's hierarchy of needs and some collateral research

LEVEL	MASLOW	KOHLBERG	LOEVINGER
6	**Self-actualization** Being that self which I truly am Being all I have it in me to be Fully functioning person Authentic Creative	**Individual principles** True personal conscience Universal principles fully internalized Genuinely autonomous Selfishness B	**Autonomous:** **integrated** Flexible and creative Internal conflicts are faced and recognized Tolerance for ambiguity Respect for autonomy
5	**Esteem 2** Goals founded on self- evaluated standards Self-confidence	**Social contract** Utilitarian law-making Principles of general welfare Long-term goals	**Conscientious** Bound by self-imposed rules Differentiated thinking Self-aware

THE GREAT GAP

LEVEL	MASLOW	KOHLBERG	LOEVINGER
4	**Esteem 1** Respect from others Social status Recognition	**Law and order** Authority maintenance Fixed social rules Find duty and do it	**Conformist 2** Seeking general rules of social conformity Justifying conformity
3	**Love & belongingness** Wish for affection Need for acceptance Need for tenderness	**Personal** **concordance** Good-boy morality Seeking social approval Liking to be liked	**Conformist 1** Going along with the crowd Anxiety about rejection Need for support
2	**Effectance** Mastery Imposed control Blame and retaliation Domination	**Instrumental** **hedonism** Naive egocentrism Horse-trading approach Profit-and-loss calculation Selfishness A	**Self-protective** Wary and exploitative People are means to ends Competitive stance Fear of being caught
1	**Safety** Defence against danger Fight or flight Fear: world is a scary place	**Obedience/** **Punishment** Deference to superior power Rules are external and eternal Musts and shoulds	**Impulsive** Domination by immediate cue, body feelings No reflection

After David Wright (1973), omitting lowest level of Maslow (physiological) and Loevinger
(pre-social, symbiotic).

continues overleaf

Figure 1 Maslow and levels.

Maslow's hierarchy of needs and some collateral research

LEVEL	PIAGET	ALDERFER	WILBER
6	**Dialectical operations** (Klaus Riegel 1984) Beyond formal logic Integration of contradictions	**Growth**	**Centaur 2** Vision-logic Bodymind integration Peak experiences Existential self
5	**Formal operations** Substage 2: Thinking about thinking Forethought, speculation	**Growth**	**Centaur 1** Ecological imagination Awareness of awareness Relative autonomy

THE GREAT GAP

LEVEL	PIAGET	ALDERFER	WILBER
4	**Formal operations** Substage 1: Capacity for hypothetico-deductive thinking	**Relatedness**	**Mental ego** Full rationality Syllogistic logic Science/mathematics
3	**Concrete operations** Ability to take role of other	**Relatedness**	**Mythic-membership** Dependent on roles Norm-dominated
2	**Preoperational** Mastery Incapable of seriation	**Existence**	**Magical** Primary process thinking High credulity
1	**Sensoriphysical**	**Existence**	**Body ego** Archaic level of thought

Figure 1 (continued)

groups. Being real simply means not hiding behind our roles and the expectations we have adopted without noticing: our unaware "shoulds". In personal growth groups we say what we mean and mean what we say. We see out of our own eyes, rather than out of the eyes of others. We take full responsibility for what we say and do. Learning how to do this is often harder than we thought at first it would be, and group work is ideally suited to help in this. It works by confronting us with the task, and supporting us in carrying it out. This combination of support and confrontation is crucial to group work, as Peter Smith's (1973) classic work has shown.

What is personal growth?

There are really two main kinds of personal growth groups, in terms of the people who go to them. Firstly there are groups which people go to entirely off their own initiative, for their own satisfaction. We are not concerned with that here.

Secondly there are the personal growth groups which are part of a course in counselling or psychotherapy, often called personal development or PD groups. Here the person is required to go to the group to enhance the personal development that is expected to take place on such a course. It would not be right, the reasoning goes, to try to counsel other people if one had done no work on oneself. Some of the blocks to being one's self can be worked through in individual therapy, but there are some which cannot. For example, if someone talks too much, this is never going to come out as a problem in individual therapy, but it will emerge straight away in a group. These groups are often a humbling experience, which demonstrate convincingly to people that they are not as ready to become counsellors as they had thought at first. In all cases those attending are not called "patients" but rather "participants" or "group members".

The people who lead such groups are counsellors or psychotherapists who have taken specific training in group work, and are experienced at working in this way. They are usually in supervision, but in privately run groups there is no guarantee of this. If this is a concern, it is easy enough to ask about it.

The general point to be made about personal growth groups is that there is no assumption made in these that people are sick or inferior or defective in any way. As can be seen very easily in the Maslow model, it is more a question of following a developmental path a bit further than most people bother to do. The journey begins with the permission and encouragement to be real. Then quite a number of specific approaches are mobilized in the search for further helps in crossing the great gap.

Groups are also used, and this is our main concern here, as an approach to individual psychotherapy.

Jacob Moreno (see Karp et al. 1998) was one of the pioneers of this direction. Through the method of psychodrama which he developed Moreno showed how people could be helped to be more creative and spontaneous than they had been before. In psychodrama people can re-enact scenes from their past with the help of other group members. Each member takes different roles; for example, that of their father, or mother, or a previous teacher. The member then acts as if they were that figure. This is clearly turning the real person of past or present existence into an I-position. Group members can also see themselves acted out by others. Each member can then change their current responses to others in their daily lives, or see other possibilities of getting out of old and apparently impossible situations. Personification can be used very easily in this context, as it is possible not only to confront other group members, but also parents, teachers, and parts of oneself, such as one's depression, one's tiredness, or procrastination, or anger. Peter Pitzele, working with adolescents, often uses a simple structure:

"I do this with two chairs, one placed behind the other. The first chair is for the mask, the second chair is for whatever might be going on behind it" (Pitzele 1991, p.18). Each of these has become an I-position.

In this approach, other people in the group may come forward to represent whatever might be on the back chair. Or someone else may sit on the front chair and the protagonist may sit behind and play the intrapsychic role. There are many variations that may be played. The language of I-positions is very helpful in seeing how this is a unified process throughout.

The dialogical self

In relation to the dialogical self, an important contribution has come from the psychodramatist Leni Verhofstadt-Denève in Belgium. She has elaborated a model which is of considerable use and interest, using concepts such as the self-image, the alter-image and the meta-self. Each of these has an actual version and an ideal version. These six positions form a therapeutically practicable and living personality model, and she points out that "the reflection of the I on the Me is more comprehensive than the conventional self-reflection, since the Me contains not merely the self, but also the whole social and object world" (Verhofstadt-Denève 2003, p.185).

She makes it clear that there may be interdimensional conflicts, intra-dimensional oppositions and possible alternative constructions. And she uses Moreno's concept of the "social atom" (someone's social network of significant others) in her research.

She makes the point that "Action techniques, however, are much more than simple action tricks. They must be grounded in an appropriate theory of personality and personality development" (Verhofstadt-Denève 2003, p.194). And she quotes Hermans (2001) to show the kind of theory she is thinking of. She closes by saying that "All this means that dialogical self-processes can be strongly supported and intensified if the person as a multivoiced self is given the opportunity to move effectively (in the words of Hermans 2001) from one I-position to the others, in order to really meet and become the antagonists in a concrete time and space experience" (Verhofstadt-Denève 2003, p.197).

Carl Rogers (see Kirschenbaum & Henderson 1990) was another pioneer, insisting that a growth group had to be person-centred in the sense of helping people to find who they really are instead of having fixed aims for them. People in person-centred groups are encouraged to give up the masks they generally use to get by in social interactions. Instead, each member is enabled and supported in expressing directly and genuinely the feelings that arise for them in the group. Rogers' emphasis on genuineness, empathy, and acceptance has influenced many other approaches to counselling and to psychotherapy. A useful summary chart is given in the chapter by Fred Zimring (see Figure 2).

Maslow chart levels 3–4 ("ME")	Maslow chart levels 5–6 ("I")
Socially defined self	Personally defined self
Behaviour guided by incorporated social standards	Goals set by own values
Morality defined by society	Morality based on personal values
Agenda for what has to be done set by society	Agenda set by self
Enables problem solution according to social standards	New, creative solutions
Repository of social knowledge and expectations	Contains self-knowledge
Provides social viewpoint in line with assimilated social values, attitudes and interactions	Reacts creatively to "me"
Passive recipient or reactive self	Proactive
Concerned with past and future	Experiencing the present
Focus on others	Focus on self
Lives in roles	Acts from present personal values
Negative feelings and distress occur as a result of judgement of others	Distress occurs as a result of not meeting own goals

Figure 2 I and me.

Source: Adapted from Zimring (2001), p.92.

A third name that must be mentioned is that of Fritz Perls (see Clarkson & Mackewn 1993). Perls developed Gestalt therapy and emphasized awareness and personal presence. He insisted on paying attention to the how (rather than the why) and the now (rather than the past or future). Perls encouraged paying attention to unfinished cycles of making contact with people, and to the splits we create to disrupt such cycles. An example can be to apologize whenever the cycle would call for expressing anger. In this case the cycle of contact is disrupted by splitting the expression of anger from the expression of appreciation. He also developed ways of enabling group members to intensify the aspects they split; for example, expressing appreciation more intensely and then expressing anger more loudly. By shuttling between the two extremes, a new resolution emerges. Fritz Perls' contribution was basic to the theory of paradoxical change (Beisser 1972) that has been adopted in many other areas of counselling and of psychotherapy.

As must be obvious, personification can be used very freely in a Gestalt group. We can not only personify people, but also such entities as a car number-plate, water pouring out of a jug, "your smirk", and so forth. Each of these can become an I-position, limited only by the creativity of the therapist.

We do need help to begin crossing the gap. Up until the Great Gap, society gives a great deal of support and help in ascending the Maslovian hierarchy of needs. It may even sometimes feel like being carried up on an escalator. But at the point where the Great Gap begins, society ceases to encourage us, and we have to carry on by ourselves, under our own steam. We have to become more autonomous in order to progress at all. That is where these types of growth group come in. In this sense there is a sort of paradox about growth groups: we join them to become more autonomous, yet we have to be a little bit autonomous in order to take the risk of joining such a group.

A range of types

Shaffer and Galinsky (1989) offer the best account of the range of groups that have been developed over the years. They describe: the social work group (support groups, educational groups, groups for empowerment and even self-help groups); the psychoanalytic therapy group (the group-analytic group from Foulkes, the Tavistock group, the group-dynamic group, the Wolf and Schwartz type group, the Whitaker and Lieberman group and so on); the existential-experiential group (Hora, Mullen and Berger are specifically mentioned); psychodrama (the powerful and widely influential group developed by Moreno); the Gestalt therapy workshop (owing to Fritz Perls); cognitive-behaviour therapy in groups (desensitization, imagery work, assertiveness training, many techniques from Albert Ellis, Meichenbaum's work and so on); T-Groups and the laboratory method (the most unstructured of all the groups mentioned here, stimulating research which led to the generally accepted sequence of stages in a group); the encounter group (Rogers, Schutz and so forth – perhaps the most flexible of all the group approaches, in the hands of a well-trained and experienced facilitator); the theme-centred interactional method (from Ruth Cohn); and the self-help group (well described in the wonderful book by Ernst & Goodison 1981). In each case they give a general introduction and historical background, an illustration of a typical session, key concepts and special techniques, and the role of the facilitator. Of course at the time that they wrote there was no concept of the dialogical self, which would have been so useful to them.

Any of these groups can be used for personal growth, although this is not always the case. In practice the two main approaches in this country are the person-centred group developed by Carl Rogers in the USA, and naturalized into the UK by people like Brian Thorne, Dave Mearns and Tony Merry, and the group-analytic group developed by Sigmund Heinrich Foulkes in

Britain. The person-centred group is most similar to the encounter group or the existential-experiential group as described by Shaffer and Galinsky, and comes from the humanistic camp. The group-analytic group is most similar to the psychoanalytic group as described by Shaffer and Galinsky, and is often described as a psychodynamic group. There are other types of group on offer in some locations, such as psychodrama groups, which are in most cases excellent now, because the training has become quite rigorous in recent years. Gestalt groups are also now mostly run by well-trained people, and are a very good source for use in training. Tavistock groups are not so good for personal growth, and are of more use to people working in organizations who want to deal with their fantasies about authority figures.

We must not forget the self-help group. People who want to embark on a programme of self-development often find in this a way of doing the work they need to do without spending large sums of money. Sheila Ernst and Lucy Goodison (1981) have written an excellent text on this, which gives a great deal of information about starting up and running such a group. Personification is used very freely and effectively here. Co-counselling (Kauffman & New 2004) is a way of working in a one-to-one way, though groups are also used. In the groups, I-positions are used very freely and creatively. A brief training course is involved, but after that the procedure is free. The women's movement developed a variety of consciousness-raising groups. The men's movement has included various forms of groups where men explore how to change and develop new gender identities and gender roles (Rowan 1997). A useful approach comes from the group labelled "Navigator" by James Traeger and his colleagues (Traeger et al. 2006). This is very interesting work, which is becoming used more in organizations.

Aiming at the whole person

Personal growth groups, in the sense of groups that did not assume any pathology, started in the 1960s as part of what was called the growth movement. They often took place in growth centres such as the Esalen Institute in California or the Open Centre in London, both of which still exist. The idea was that all the techniques used in psychotherapy, and new ones too, could also be used simply for the benefit of ordinary people with no particular illnesses or defects. They could then develop further, and leave behind their compulsions, unconsidered assumptions and unexamined values, and ascend the Maslovian ladder. They could grow to become what Carl Rogers used to call "a fully-functioning person", or "that self which I truly am" – what Maslow called the self-actualized person. Nowadays the number of growth centres has diminished, but the approach is more wide-spread than ever, forming part of virtually every course in counselling and psychotherapy which aims at authenticity. Counsellors and psychotherapists, more than most, need to be whole persons, as authenticity demands, and as Jung (1966) pointed out long ago. And in exploring these issues, personification is of great use, because it is a very effective way of looking at what Jung calls the Shadow – the part of ourselves which we like least and maybe know least about. In a dream, for example, if the dreamer seems to be chased by a fearsome pursuer, the therapist may suggest taking the role of the aggressor, as a possibly important part of the dreamer's Shadow. Much can be discovered by turning the pursuer into an I-position. A client who often takes up a victim role can discover many new and valuable things about themselves by taking up the I-position of the aggressor in the dream.

Some key issues

Generally speaking, psychodynamic groups have lower horizons, and have more restricted aims. They are more oriented toward adjustment and coping, and therefore come more under the instrumental rubric. But some of them, with a more eclectic approach, do seem a bit more ambitious. So far as personal growth in the psychodynamic group is concerned, one of the best discussions is to be found in the chapter by Wolf and Kutash (1986). They go into the interesting question, for example, of how things can go wrong in such groups.

Some of the important issues which arise in groups are trust, safety and confrontation.

Trust

Trust influences learning, because we have to trust a communication to some degree before we can even hear it, never mind learn from it. Trust influences cooperation, because it is hard to cooperate with someone if we do not trust them. Trust influences getting along with others, establishing friendships and inspiring the confidence of one's peers.

Trust is just as important in a group as it is in individual therapy, but it is actually harder to achieve. It is important in both cases because we cannot open up to another person if we do not trust them. Risking (very necessary in a good group) and trusting go hand in hand. It is often beneficial to explore trust by using personification – bringing into the room old situations and possible new situations involving trust.

In a group, if no one takes any risks, stagnation can easily result. But mistrust can get in the way of risking anything. However, there is a paradox here. There is no way of proving that anyone is trustworthy: so we are always going to have to go beyond the evidence if we are going to get anywhere at all. It there is no way of ever proving finally that a person or group is trustworthy, we may as well take a risk and find out that way. So in order to engender trust, we have to act as if we trusted even if we do not trust. We have to risk if we are going to create trust. Then a two-way interaction can start up between trust and cooperation, and the whole group can come alive.

Trusting behaviour influences risk-taking. This is the basic point. To test whether someone is trustworthy involves taking some kind of risk. This testing goes on more at the beginning of a relationship than later on, but it can be renewed at any point where trust wavers. Perceived trustworthiness makes everything easier. Reliance on the words or actions of another is never total, nor should it be, because that way lies disappointment and disillusion. But openness is certainly to be aimed at: partly because it is one of the goals of group work in terms of personal growth. This means the owning of behaviour, and taking responsibility for our own actions, or in other words authenticity. Less important in the end are our expectations of what others will do. The door to cooperation can only be opened from our side. We cannot expect someone else to do it for us.

Safety

Often at the beginning of a group people are a little scared of what might happen in the group. The customary reassurance about confidentiality and no violence in the group does not go very far to allay their fears. But really the best answer to this is given by Starhawk (1987), when she says: "Safety in a group is not a matter of niceness or politeness . . . But a group can establish safety by assuring that risks are shared, that boundaries are clear, and that power structures and hidden agendas are brought out into the open. We cannot eliminate risks, but we can face them with solidarity" (Starhawk 1987, p.145). It is part of the role of the group facilitator to hold the boundaries of the group, and to ensure that important issues are not ignored or glossed over. Again personification can be used to explore safety by bringing in "unsafe" figures of one kind or another, and then taking up that role oneself.

Confrontation

Confrontation (sometimes also called challenging) has to be well handled if it is to be fruitful. It is best done in the spirit of accurate empathy, really trying to get into the other person's shoes before speaking. It should be tentative rather than dogmatic. It should be done with care, meaning that there should be some real involvement with the other person. It should be done with attention to your own motivation: Is it really for the other person's benefit, or for your own benefit? Use real or authentic communication so that the message comes from your own self and your own experience, not from some pseudo objectivity (Egan 1976). One handy slogan that emphasizes real communication and how to achieve it is: "Use giraffe language, not jackal language". Giraffe language is always a description of what is happening inside you: it is a kind of owning up. The giraffe is the animal with the biggest heart in the jungle. Jackal language attacks the other person by labelling, by blaming, by questioning, by preaching . . . – all those types of communication which distance us from the other person and make them defensive.

Personification and role-playing can be very useful in exploring these issues.

Also important in a group is the way in which you respond to confrontation: try not to be defensive. Let in the communication, and make sure you understand it – ask questions if necessary to clarify what is being said, and listen to the answers.

This openness now begins to remind us of the transpersonal, which we shall meet more fully in the next chapter; but let us just look at a couple of examples of using personification in a transpersonal way in groups.

When Will Schutz tells the story of a British woman in one of his groups who was asked to become very small and go inside her own body (Shaffer & Galinsky 1989, p.218), he was working in a way calculated to enable transpersonal energies to enter in. It is clear that imagery very often involves playing with the normal limitations of time and space. (In his 1980s work, Schutz (1981) explicitly uses meditation, prayer, chanting and Arica spiritual exercises.)

Jim Elliott does not say as much as Schutz about the spiritual aspects of his work, but he does say that human beings are not just physical objects but are best characterized by such words as freedom, choice, growth, autonomy and mystery. These are all characteristics of transpersonal work. He also refers to creativity and liberation (Elliott 1976, p.58).

Creativity, too, is one of the areas which may have to do with the superconscious as described by Assagioli (Ferrucci 1982). A good group leader will not only be creative himself, but will stimulate the creativity in other people.

Another phenomenon noted by Elliott is the Fusion Experience, which often happens after primals and similar cathartic experiences. The whole person is involved, and seems often taken outside their ordinary world. "Looking back on the experience, [one has] the feeling that one was outside time and space. Typical comments are 'The world fell away' . . ." (Elliott 1976, p.198). This is the kind of peak experience which is very characteristic of transpersonal work.

Elizabeth Mintz does not say much about spirituality in her 1972 book, but makes up for it by a later book which is all about it. In this book she gives an example where a young man's impotence was cured, not by the usual process of therapy, but by a group ritual in which he symbolically castrated each of the other men in the group. This arose quite spontaneously in the group, and she says of the event: "It was an enactment of a mythic ritual, a primitive ceremony, which tapped the deep levels of the collective unconscious; it was a transpersonal experience" (Mintz 1983, pp.153–157). This is not to say that everything describable as mythic must be transpersonal, as Ken Wilber has pointed out at length in his essay on the pre-trans fallacy (Wilber 1983).

In the same book, Mintz talks of countertransference of such a kind that the group leader actually feels inside her own body the next thing which needs to happen for the participant. This links directly with the research on countertransference mentioned by Andrew Samuels (1989), which again links this with the transpersonal, and with the Jungian idea of the imaginal world.

It is my strong impression that the climate has changed considerably since the early 1980s, in the direction of more open acknowledgement of the importance of the transpersonal. It was always important in encounter, but it is only more recently that people have said so very much. In the next chapter we shall see how this developed.

Part III

Directions and the potential

Chapter 8

The transpersonal

The conventional wisdom is that I-positions are at a lower level than the real self, the soul and the spirit. They speak of imperfection and the need for further therapeutic work to resolve them or reduce them to colourful facets of a basically unified psyche. I have no quarrel with that: it is the fruit of long and reliable experience in therapy.

Let's pretend

But supposing we simply ignored all that and treated the real self, the soul and the spirit *as if* they were I-positions, what then? After all, from a therapeutic point of view, the way that I-positions are used is to put them out and talk to them. The client is asked to imagine that the I-position is sitting on a chair or cushion, in the manner explained in psychodrama, psychosynthesis, Gestalt therapy or voice dialogue, and to engage in a dialogue with that person. Why should we not equally be able to ask the client to imagine that the real self, the soul or the spirit is there on the chair?

When we experiment in this way we find that it is perfectly possible to do this. It is even possible, we find, to set up dialogues between these entities, should we so wish. And from this work some interesting findings emerge.

1   The nature of each entity is clarified by enabling borders and bound-aries to be set and a set of contrasts to emerge.
2   People find they are able to enter into states of consciousness which they previously thought could only emerge after years of spiritual practice. These states are temporary rather than permanent ("states are free, stages have to be earned") but they are quite real and useful.
3   By exploring these different levels of consciousness in this way, therapists can extend their range and expand their awareness of what is possible.

That is the basic case I am arguing here. Here is an example:
    The client was in his forties and had a lifelong interest in football. He had

a dream in which his mother was saying a number of foolish things in the presence of Sir Alex Ferguson. He was worried that Ferguson would get impatient with her. But the great man was kind, thoughtful and wise. He treated his mother with great dignity and respect. My client was very impressed with his gentle yet strong demeanour.

Without talking about it, I put out a cushion and invited my client to imagine that the Alex Ferguson of his dream was sitting on it, and he could talk to him – tell him things, ask him things, anything at all. He found this very easy, and asked him for his advice on some of the things we had been talking about earlier in the session. Then I invited him to sit on the cushion himself and speak as Alex Ferguson. He did so, and said some very wise and deep things, showing a level of depth and insight which he had never demonstrated before. I then asked him to go back to his place and be himself again. I asked him how he felt about that experience. He spoke very slowly and surely, and seemed to have gotten a lot from it.

I told him that in my opinion he had been talking to his Higher Self or Inner Teacher – someone who he could now contact at any time. This was a figure who could be a resource for him when in doubt. He left feeling much better, he said, about the problems he had been going into earlier. We can also think of this figure as representing his soul – the wisest part of himself – or his psychic centre, as Cortright (2007) has urged, following Aurobindo.

This is what I was saying in 2003:

> In the whole field of therapy there are three great realms, which can be labelled as the instrumental, the authentic and the transpersonal. If we look at the numbers involved, probably most of the work is done at the instrumental level, a smaller amount at the authentic level, and a smaller amount again at the transpersonal level. But in terms of the level of consciousness of the therapist, although most may be located for the most part at the instrumental level, quite a large proportion are probably at the authentic level, because of the work they have done on themselves in their own therapy, and quite a decent proportion are probably at the transpersonal level, again because of their own attempts at self-development through meditation, psychosynthesis, shamanic or Tantric workshops or other practices.
>
> Subpersonality work is mostly carried out at the instrumental level, because it is here that subpersonalities give most trouble. They are usually unexamined parts of the person which cause problems because they are hidden from view. As soon as they come out into the open, and start to relate to the rest of the personality, they lose their sting and their power. And in fact to discover and deal with them is one of the best ways of moving on to the authentic stage, where we do not need them any more.

> *When we work with I-positions, the technique which helps most is concretization. This can be done in various ways: through two-chair work, through art work, through Voice Dialogue, through psychosynthesis, through active imagination, through work with dolls or sandplay, and so on. Perhaps the most common of these is two-chair work, because it is very flexible and easily adapted.*
>
> *What we are going to do in this workshop is to adapt two-chair work to a job for which it was never intended, in order to push the boundaries and to try something original.*

So clearly something new was being envisaged here, although it had been suggested earlier by others, for example Will Parfitt from the psychosynthesis school, who gives us this exercise:

> Relax and centre.
>
> Sit on a chair or cushion with a second chair or cushion conveniently placed in front of you, facing in your direction. Imagine that your soul sits on that chair. Without trying too hard, engage your soul in a dialogue. Start by telling it something about what you think, feel or sense.
>
> When you feel ready, move positions, sit on the chair or cushion opposite and become your soul. Look back at yourself as a personality in the original position, and answer back. Say whatever comes to you.
>
> At your own pace, allow a dialogue to happen between your personality and your soul. Do not try to make it anything special, or force it in any way, but simply see what happens. And watch for non-verbal messages that might come from the soul chair, such as particular body postures, facial expressions, gestures and so on.
>
> (Parfitt 1990, p.122)

His is not a scholarly book, because there are few indications of where the various things come from: it is a practical book for wide use. It is as if the author were saying: I have been working in this field for some time, and here are some of the best things I have come across and used myself.

Another person who has also used this idea is Molly Young Brown, also from the psychosynthesis school, who uses the symbol of the Wise Person to represent the soul, and encourages the client to write a letter to the Wise Person: "Writing can be useful in seeking answers from the superconscious and in opening ourselves to new perspectives" (Brown 2004, p.148). In an earlier book she had suggested writing a letter to the Self (Brown 1993, p.42). I found this quite ambiguous, as to whether it was to be addressed to the soul (Subtle level) or to the spirit (Causal level) – the Self as a concept used in psychosynthesis I find unclear on this distinction, which as we shall see is so important in psychotherapy.

In the field of coaching, Sir John Whitmore has suggested that the psychosynthesis approach is very valuable (Whitmore & Einzig 2007). And he has shown that even hardened executives can be shown how to use such concepts.

If we agree that we all have I-positions, and that there can be dialogues between them, that is all quite clear and fine. But is that all? If there is an authentic self, as would be required in an existential construction, how is that to be conceptualized and treated? If there is a soul, as a transpersonal construction would have it, how is that to be conceptualized and treated? And if we recognize the Spirit, how is that to be conceptualized and treated? I want to urge the dialectical solution of saying that the authentic self is and is not an I-position, that the soul is and is not an I-position, that the spirit is and is not an I-position. The meaning is in the movement, in the sense that by grasping the dialectical notion of paradox we can move forward in psychotherapy without denying the reality and importance of the authentic self, the soul and the spirit. The therapist and the client both gain in freedom from this acceptance of a paradoxical reality.

When I used these ideas in workshops they became very concrete and practical. Let us just see what the results were, in terms of the actual experience of the participants.

What comes out

One report said that the workshop started by outlining Ken Wilber's four levels of Mental Ego or instrumental self, Centaur or authentic self, Subtle or transpersonal self 1, and Causal or transpersonal self 2. It was explained that an individual can experience development within a particular level of consciousness (translation) or a more significant and fundamental move from one level to another (transformation). If we move from one level to another, this type of growth revises our whole sense of who we are.

There was then an exercise to give these different levels a voice, the first one being to write a dialogue between the Centaur or authentic self and the Subtle or transpersonal self 1, or soul. A handout was given to help in this, along the lines of the chart in Chapter 4. One participant said:

> My "conversation" did not proceed fluently. At least as dialogue it did not. As a monologue it proceeded apace. My authentic self, confident in its established position as the way to be was strong in its competence and advantages. My subtle self, while feeling that it should be more developed after all its years of Christian nurturing, found itself surprisingly mute and uncertain of who it was.
>
> Comparing our experiences in pairs I had no problem in locating myself on the psychospiritual map and identifying the focus of my growth as translation within the level of the authentic self. The weak voice of my

subtle self had surprised me as it had the Buddhist with whom I was comparing notes. Perhaps we were not as spiritually developed as we might have thought.

This shows the paradox inherent in this sort of work. On the one hand the task seems easy and straightforward, but on the other hand there may be unexpected difficulties and resistances.

Out of this kind of work came a chart which I have found useful in practice. In two columns, it contrasts the authentic self with the soul, as can be seen in Figure 3.

After a break, the next exercise was to set about allowing the two transpersonal selves – the "subtle" and the "causal" – to converse. Again a handout was provided, along the lines of the chart. Again we can look at the experience of a participant:

The causal self includes the following characteristics: no interest in symbols, no interest in gender, sees through distinctions between unity and diversity, paradox runs through everything, one with nature, no fear because nothing is alien. It was the voice of this self that indulged its opportunity to speak. Full of discontent at being discounted and unappreci-ated and whose only consolation seemed to be biding its time until it would come into its own in eternity. I was both surprised and amused at the strength of feeling.

Following each of the two conversations I demonstrated a brief counsellor–client encounter. This was to show how different the experience would be with the counsellor meeting the client with a different self. Volunteer clients emerged. I met the first as my subtle self and later the second as my causal self. Participants said that it was surprising what a very different "feel" this gave to these most brief of meetings. It also seemed to lead to a very different experience for the two "clients".

Out of these experiences another chart emerged, this time contrasting the subtle with the causal, as shown in Figure 4.

Later in the year I presented another workshop, with a somewhat different title, which brought in the question of transpersonal levels but did not explicitly mention subpersonalities or I-positions. Again I started by outlining the Wilber theory, and pointed out that the implication of his work was that self-actualization was quite achievable, rather than being the remote goal which in the 1970s it had seemed to be. I did a demonstration with a volunteer of work at the authentic level, just to set the base level at which a great deal of work in therapy is carried out.

We then went on to the Subtle level, again helped with a demonstration. One participant said:

Authentic self	Soul
Separate	Connected
Clear perception	Love
Likes boundaries	Not much interested in boundaries
Thinks in words, likes imagery	Thinks in imagery, suspicious of words
Uses dialectical way of thinking	Uses intuitive way of thinking
Can use symbols	Immersed in symbols
Interested in people	Interested in people, animals, plants . . .
The divine may be out there	The divine can be in here
Understanding is the most important thing	Imagination is the most important thing
Interested in knowing	Interested in not-knowing
Thoughtful compassion	Emotional compassion
Finds self in contrast to other	Finds self in other
Creative	Surrendered, inspired
Trees can be beautiful	Trees can be devas (nature spirits)
Has internal gyroscope	Has daimon (genius, angel, inner teacher)
Good at psychotherapy	Good at mental healing
In touch with the body	In touch with the subtle body
Has many skills	Waits for guidance
In touch with own authentic self	In touch with the divine
Steers clear of magic	Can use magic with divine guidance
Uses experiential knowing	Uses intuition
Creativity comes from inside	Creativity comes from outside inspiration
Ecstasy is personal	Ecstasy is divine
Clear about boundaries	Can allow boundaries to disappear
Not much interest in mythology	Steeped in mythology, fairy tales, etc.
Sees what is visible	Sees what is invisible
Interested in bodymind energy	Interested in subtle energy

Figure 3 Authentic self and soul.

Soul/subtle	Spirit/causal
Fascinated by symbols	No interest in symbols
Concerned with gender	No concern with gender
Polytheistic	Monotheistic or nontheistic
Juicy compassion	Constant clear compassion
Knows many techniques	Invents techniques as necessary
Deep linking with the other	No need for distinction between self and other
Interested in angels and auras	No interest in such things
Values diversity	Sees through distinction between unity and diversity
Fascinated by paradox	Paradox runs through everything
Values the third eye	Rises above the third eye
Focused on many beings	Focused on Being
Concern to build up resources	Infinite resources without concern
Creative approach to problems	No concept of a problem
Deeply identified with Nature	One with Nature
Can relate to trees as devas	Is all the trees in the world, and all the tree-cutters too, and the no-tree
Has compassion for the unfortunate	Has compassion for the unfortunate and for the fortunate
Wants the World Soul to be well and happy and free from suffering	Knows that the World Soul is already well and happy and free from suffering
Wants to save what was lost	No one has lost everything
Unafraid of what is alien	No fear because nothing is alien
Rejoices in the Many	One-ing
Rejoices in the rich taste of all	There is nothing to taste, and no one to taste it. Or perhaps there is just one taste.

Figure 4 Subtle versus Causal.

We had a discussion of this level too and the most important thing that emerged was a feeling of having passed through an "either/or" consciousness to a "both/and" level of being. As we discussed the Subtle level of our thinking, our "being" also shifted into the Subtle level by virtue of common sympathies, some kind of osmosis took place. I have also noticed the difference of levels of ease amongst the participants, as some were showing signs of strain and challenge being drawn to this level, whilst others were very much in their elements.

Then came a lunch break and after lunch I introduced the last column. Some people seemed to have come mainly for this: something that they had met in their spiritual development, but had not thought to use in therapy. One participant said:

I was eager to volunteer to be the client for this demonstration. John started with a minute or so of silent meditation. I was very nervous at first, this was the first time I have revealed this part of myself in front of an audience. As soon as I started speaking the room seemed to have disappeared and there was only John and me. Within minutes I felt relieved as I felt John was truly there with me, not as John, but something impersonal and at the same time deeply familiar, and I was no longer "me" but something that was acutely aware of the interaction and the presence. I was left with a sense of great gratitude. It was very meaningful for me, although it was hard for lots of people to follow what was going on. This new level of being and relating didn't feel like therapy at all and it was very different again from the previous levels of therapy.

There were some short questions after the demonstration, people were trying to find some foothold, some experience in their own lives that related to this nebulous, intangible stage. I saw people deeply immersed in contemplation, in inner search. The energy stilled and quieted. Next I suggested that participants tried for themselves either the Subtle level or the Causal level of therapy, in couples, ten minutes each being therapist and then client. One participant said:

I chose to work at the Causal level with a partner who also felt he wanted to try this. This again was quite a revelation. I did things that I don't normally do in my sessions with clients. In fact I did very little, yet it felt completely appropriate. I have improvised and just "went with the flow". I did not stand in the way in any way and we both felt that it was a powerful and meaningful joining. The use of words for description in this part of my report actually feels quite awkward, they don't quite do justice to what I'm trying to describe.

There was another brief break and then I handed out reading lists of recommended books on each level. There was a discussion where the emphasis was all on the transpersonal issues and questions. People began to disclose more and more spiritual aspects and related experiences about themselves, slowly and reluctantly at first, and more and more in depth as the discussion progressed. Unfortunately we were running out of time just as some very interesting notions were aired about God and the spiritual arena.

What I learned from this was something I had not been sure of before: that most practitioners (and I think that the attending participants were mostly humanistic or integrative in their orientation) have had some experience of the transpersonal, and can move into the appropriate states of consciousness without too much difficulty.

The next thing I did, in early 2004, was to run a short (one morning) Masterclass on authentic relating. Here there was no mention either of I-positions or of the transpersonal, although again I thought it useful to use Wilber's ideas to argue that self-actualization was experience – near, rather than some distant and perhaps unachievable goal. Again I gave a demonstration of work at the authentic level, and then asked a volunteer therapist to work with a volunteer client at that stage.

This then prepared the way for the next workshops to be more oriented towards the integration of the I-positions idea with the development of therapists in the transpersonal realms. Later in the year I was doing demonstrations of work at the Causal and even at the Nondual level, and there seemed to be no limit to where participants could go when they tried it themselves.

The work on differences between the Causal and the Nondual was particularly interesting, as this is little written about in the literature. In Figure 5 we can see how this came out.

This is very interesting, as it reveals just the kinds of contrasts that emerge in the formal literature of mysticism. The items are perhaps biased in the direction of Zen rather than Advaita, because of my particular interests, experiences and history. For a more measured example, Figure 6 shows a similar set of contrasts taken from the work of Ken Wilber.

Of course, these are rather recondite matters, and not relevant to everyone. So let us now have a look as the ways in which these ideas about the transpersonal can be used in practice.

Using these ideas in everyday therapy

What emerges from all this is that we can use these ideas in everyday therapy without enormous efforts in retraining. To the extent that we have had at least some experience of the subtle level, we can tune into this for the one hour in which we are seeing a client. Or at least we can recognize the

Causal	Nondual
The Dance of Being	It's not at the end of any continuum
No desires	No such thing as a desire
Eternal infinite selfing	Nothing needed
Not the peace of ignoring everything, but the peace of embracing everything	Who indeed?!
No need to get attached to Freedom, either	Laughter . . . Laughing . . .
There is no portal! I am already there! I have always been already there!	Ecstasy doesn't need an experiencer
The Clarity and the Mystery are one and the same	Not this, not that – and not NOT, either!
Steady breath of compassion	Not about altered states of consciousness – no one here to be conscious!
One-ing . . .	. . . Already given up long ago . . .
The Inner Light and the Inner Dark are one and the same	The brightness of the fog
Just this. Just this.	Two onions and a piece of string
Of course I am God! Of course I am not God!	What do you mean – "God"?
What ecstasy!	What ecstasy?
The Earth is empty!	What Earth?
It's all here! Nothing is missing!	Eleven fingers
No fear, because nothing is alien	The sun in the mud
Compassion flows freely	Blood runs uphill exploding
The centre is everywhere	What centre?
Can't explain it	Not the slightest need to explain it
I insist on the absence of categories	No need to insist on anything
No fear	No one to be afraid of anything
Thou Art That!	What?
Meditation is the way	Meditation is a pile of dead leaves in the driveway
Paradox is an important key	Paradox, schmaradox!

continues

Figure 5 Causal versus Nondual.

Causal	Nondual
Big Mind	Big Joke
The biggest prison of all	What prison?
It's all there!	Where?
At last! It all makes sense	At last! It all makes nonsense
Mu	Moo!

Figure 5 (continued)

state of consciousness when it comes up spontaneously in therapy. All of us have more acquaintance with the Subtle than we thought at first. After all, as Wilber has often argued, we all have dreams, and dreams are a spontaneous experience of the Subtle stage of consciousness.

We also have dreamless sleep, and Wilber has suggested that this may be an experience of the Formless, the spirit, the causal or even the Nondual. So none of these states of consciousness are far away or inaccessible. We know them all already. It is just a question of taking our courage in both hands and doing it.

Of course there are always dangers in anything new. One of the discoveries we can make at the Causal level, for example, is that there is no empathy there. This accounts for the sometimes insensitive and even brutal treatment handed out by gurus to their disciples. To a therapist brought up to believe that empathy is the best thing ever, this is a weird experience and even a crushing blow. But for the client who is ready for that, it may be just what is needed. And this is even more true of the Nondual, where a kind of humour creeps in and complicates the issue.

Therapy can be a huge realm of discovery including self-discovery, if we will let it be so. One of the most useful ways in which we can use the Subtle is in the interpretation of dreams. At the Subtle level we get the phenomenon of Linking, where the boundaries between therapist and client disappear altogether. This means that the therapist can actually enter into the dreamscape with the client, and be with the client in that scene. For example:

> Not knowing what else to do but trust that her imagination was taking her where she needed to go, I encouraged her to follow the experience farther. When she did so, her body became more rigid and hard, reflecting the frozen image within. I, too, travelled into the icy coldness of her dream. We remained there for a while, and then I noticed that her body started to change and relax.
>
> (Swinney 1999, p.70)

Source	Causal	Nondual
Aurobindo	Overmind	Supermind Sat-chit-ananda
Vedanta	Causal	Turiya
Vedanta	Bliss mind (Anandamayakosha)	Brahman-Atman (Turiyatita)
Adi Da	Nirvikalpa	Sahaja bhava
Alexander	Root mind Pure self	Brahman-Atman
Wilber	Formless mysticism Causal unity	Spirit and world process Nondual mysticism
Hazrat Inayat Khan	Wahdat – witness consciousness Djabrut-cessation Formless	Zat – absolute consciousness Nondual
Mahamudra	Simplicity Cessation Emptiness	One taste Form/Formless unity Non-meditation
Daniel Brown	Cessation Advanced insight	Enlightenment: A,b,c
Traditional	Nirvikalpa – cessation Jnana – Nirodh, Nirvana	Sahaja Non-meditation Bhava
Yoga Tantra	Causal consciousness Black near attainment Cessation	Clear-light emptiness
Duane Elgin	Global creativity (flow)	Global wisdom (integral)

Figure 6 Wilber on Causal and Nondual.

Source: Adapted from Wilber (2000a).

This is an example of how the therapist (who in this case had been trained in the shamanic tradition, which is one of the main Subtle disciplines) can actually enter in to the client's world and be there with the client.

The Californian contribution

I had thought I was alone in pursuing these transpersonal matters, but two or three years ago I came across a book entitled *The Sacred Mirror: Nondual wisdom and psychotherapy* (Prendergast et al. 2003). This sounded very exciting, because I had only recently seen the possibility of doing psychotherapy at the Causal level, and very tentatively at the Nondual level. I had found it very difficult to find texts about this, and in fact had only found a very few. To find a whole book about working at the Nondual level would be amazing.

But when I came to read the book I was taken aback to find that virtually none of it seemed to me to be fulfilling this promise. For example, in Dorothy Hunt's very warm and meaningful chapter, she says this:

> A couple I used to see for therapy had suffered the loss of a child. It created great stress in their lives and in their relationship. They were sitting one morning with me talking about issues in their relationship with one another – "he did-she did" sorts of things – when I found myself nearly in tears. I stopped them and inquired, "It feels to me that there is something powerful in the room that no one is talking about; do either of you know what I am referring to?" Immediately, he said, "Sadness", and his wife started to cry. When we work from openness, we feel what is here in the body of our being. Can we say that the sadness that was coming to me as the experience of being near tears was really mine or theirs? It was in the room. Sadness was moving.
>
> (p.175)

When I read that, I immediately recognized it as good work at the Subtle level. This is the level I have written about (Rowan 2005a) many times, where the intuition of the therapist comes fully into play, and the boundaries between therapist and client disappear. This is called Linking, and it is a classic Subtle-level phenomenon, also called Transcendental Empathy (Hart 2000).

Or listen to this, taken from an interview with Adyashanti by Prendergast and Krystal. Adyashanti says: "Oftentimes I'll just say, 'Did it ever occur to you that you're making all this up in your mind, this whole carnival show?'" (p.78). This seems to me an excellent example of work at the Causal level. The whole thing about the Causal level, as we have seen above, is that there is no empathy, unlike at the Subtle level where there is this Linking. Some time ago I wrote a paper entitled "Is it possible to work at the Causal level in therapy?" (Rowan 2005c). I came to the conclusion that it was, and at the same time pointed out that the practitioners who had written about this had by no means thrown off the shackles of their own original training:

> David Brazier (1995) writes with real authority about causal states, but when he does therapy it often sounds like psychodrama. Amy Mindell (1995) writes with real familiarity about causal states, but when she

does therapy it often sounds like Gestalt. A H Almaas (1988) writes very well about causal and even nondual states, but when he does therapy it often sounds like object relations. Mark Epstein (1996) has some very wise things to say about the causal, but when he does therapy it often sounds like psychoanalysis. Robert Rosenbaum (1998) is clearly familiar with causal states, but when he does therapy it often sounds like existential phenomenology. Perhaps it would be over-simplifying to say that the work they do is mostly in terms of their original training or experience, but there is certainly something like that going on.

(Rowan 2005, p.43)

Over and over again in this book I came across good examples of working at this level. In Prendergast's own chapter he says this:

Clients can more easily deconstruct these beliefs through inquiry (i.e. "Who or what is aware of this belief?" "Is this belief true?" "Who am I without it?") when they approach them from the expansive space of being. They are much more attuned with their inner knowing and natural clarity. When looking from this open space, clients are much more likely to see their limiting beliefs as meaningless constructs.

(p.105)

This is good Causal work, in my book: again, notice the absence of empathy.

Working at the Subtle level is of course much more common, as I have argued in my work on Linking (Rowan 2005a, pp.162–173) and is well known, for example, in psychosynthesis. They have a drawing in psychosynthesis of a landscape with two peaks. The sea rises up and fills the valley, and now there are two islands. The islands become very different, but it is still the same landscape, the same ground of being after all. This insight has been movingly described by Nathan Field (1996) as a "four-dimensional state", but he offers no pretensions to nondual status.

And recently the person-centred school has discovered what they call "working at relational depth" (Mearns & Cooper 2005), which they now admit is a Subtle phenomenon.

In the original book to which I had been referring (Prendergast et al. 2003) there was no acknowledgement of the existence of the Causal, but in the second book (Prendergast & Bradford 2007), this was remedied. In the "Introductory Remarks" by the editors, they quote Ken Wilber (1996) as outlining this distinction, and say that they agree with it. However, in the main body of the text, this distinction is never referred to again: nor does it appear in the index.

The most basic point is this: as long as the therapist has a relationship with the client, this must be work at the Subtle level or below. In my earlier paper, I remarked – "What is so striking is that therapists who are obviously familiar with the Causal and able to speak and write in Causal terms, usually resort to the Subtle when actually doing their work" (Rowan 2005c, p.43). At the Causal level and in the Nondual, there is no relationship – there is just clear perception and clarity. Certainly there is a kind of compassion – steady and unwavering – but there is nothing personal about it. It is just there.

Wilber speaks interestingly about the way in which the Nondual is often introduced in advanced teaching.

> In the Nondual traditions, you often get a quick introduction to the Nondual condition very early in your training. The master will simply point out that part of your awareness that is already nondual . . . Every experience you have is already nondual, whether you realize it or not. So it is not necessary for you to change your state of consciousness in order to discover this nonduality. Any state of consciousness you have will do just fine, because nonduality is fully present in every state . . . Change of state is useless, a distraction.
>
> (Wilber 2000b, pp.266–267)

Perhaps this helps to account for the way in which the Prendergast people use the term. But left as this simple denial of all difference, it amounts to no more than the dark in which all cats are grey.

With this in mind, let us look at a case example from the second book. Kenneth Bradford describes an interaction where the client tells him something about her past. He gives her a long silence, ending with the words: "Well, we'll see" (p.66). Is this an example of work at the Nondual level? Three years later, the client remembers this incident, and says – "I knew I could trust you." It is clear from this that the therapist was far from impersonal: was in fact in a rather deep relationship with the client. And as this second conversation goes on, it emerges that the therapist feels the depth of that relationship. This is not "unconditional presence" (Bradford's own term) – it is a rather deep therapeutic relationship: and as such it seems to me part of the Subtle.

In another chapter, Judith Blackstone says: "I have developed a method, called Realization Process, to help people experience nondual consciousness in the clinical setting. This is a series of exercises that attune directly to the pervasive expanse of nondual consciousness, and to the subtle core of the body as an entranceway into this dimension" (p.93). She then gives an example of her work with a client, in which it is clear that a good relationship is developing between them. This again seems to me to take us back into the Subtle.

Similarly, Dorothy Hunt gives an example where a client asked if she could explore the sensation she was calling fear was located. The example continues with an exploration, initiated by the therapist, in which the client is led to dare to explore the whole phenomenon (p.111). The relationship again is one of empathy and trust, very characteristic of work at the Subtle level.

There are plenty more examples, but perhaps that is enough to make my point that virtually all of this work is being conducted, not even at the Causal level, but at the Subtle.

One perhaps revealing quote from the book helps to sum up my dissatisfaction. Timothy Conway, in his chapter on Nondual Awakening, says: "A blend of compassionate, conventional-level psychospiritual counsel along with Absolute-level teachings seems to work best for most folks" (p.245). This bland acceptance of the unacceptable does not reassure me at all. It seems an admission that the work being done is not at the Nondual level, and sometimes not even at the Subtle.

It seems obvious to me that the Byron Katie work (referred to at times by the Prendergast group) and the Big Mind work, which is so popular at the moment, are both examples of giving people insights into the Causal level. At times they may even open up the Nondual to a few people, but to assume that they are then operating at the Nondual level seems to me a step too far.

Meeting the Shadow

Wilber deals with the question of the Shadow at some length in his 2006 book, making clear that much of the high-level writing in this field has a serious omission. He says that after 30 years of checking, he is now sure that "an understanding of psychodynamic repression, as well as ways to cure it, is something contributed exclusively by modern Western psychology" (Wilber 2006, p.119). And of course some of the writers in these Nondual books know this very well. Brian Wittine, who comes from a Jungian background and works rather obviously at a Subtle level, says "Moreover, when our needs are unmet, they remain unconsciously active but archaic and immature. There is then a lifelong need to find others to fulfil them" (Prendergast, Fenner & Krystal 2003, p.277). It seems clear to me that someone suffering from such problems needs a good ordinary therapist to deal with them, and only then will they be able to be open and available enough to deal with the radical openness of the Nondual or indeed the Causal. As Wilber says: "Painful experience has demonstrated time and again that *meditation simply will not get at the original shadow*, and can, in fact, often exacerbate it" (Wilber 2006, p.126). But the word "shadow" is not in the index of either of the two Nondual books. The problem is not recognized and not dealt with. Peter Fenner actually says:

There are three different ways through which we can receive what people are communicating to us: positive listening, negative listening, and pure listening. Negative listening occurs when we listen through a filter of boredom, disinterest, invalidation, annoyance, arrogance, anger, frustration, and so on. Positive listening is marked by moods of interest, enthusiasm, excitement, approval, and validation.

(Fenner 2007, p.109)

This just ignores the typical situation where our listening is distorted without our knowledge by influences from the past of which we are unaware. This is the shadow area which these people seem completely blind to.

To sum up, then, my case is that these people are mostly talking about the extremely rare case where a client who has dealt with all their shadow stuff meets a therapist who has done the same. This may be quite marvellous, but it is obviously vanishingly rare. For the most part, what really seems to be happening is that a client who has by no means dealt with all their stuff meets a therapist who talks about the Nondual and works at the Subtle level, where psychodynamic stuff can well be dealt with properly and with a wonderfully deep sense of empathy.

For this book the point is that I-positions fit very well with work at the Subtle level, but not with work at the Causal or Nondual. And it is at the Subtle level that most of the transpersonal work is being done, whether by the Jungians, the psychosynthesis people, the person-centred people, by the Californians or anyone else.

Chapter 9

Some ways forward

How does the whole thing look, now that we can see it as a whole? The first thing is obviously that the whole field is experiencing a growth spurt of enormous proportions. The new work, much more research based than anything previously encountered, is not only very extensive, but is also very convincing and impossible to ignore.

Another point, surprisingly emerging more in the coaching field than in the more established fields of counselling and psychotherapy, is the embracing of the transpersonal. Of course it is only in recent years that we have been able to write convincingly about the transpersonal, with the work of Ken Wilber, Jorge Ferrer, Jenny Ward and many others, and the arrival of solid academic efforts such as the *Journal of Transpersonal Psychology*.

Personification in coaching

Since so much coaching is done on the telephone, it may be doubted whether personification can be used. However, it seems clear that it can. We can as coaches say things like this: "Imagine that you are talking to your boss. Try saying what you really feel, irrespective of how your boss might react in real life. This is for your benefit, not for his at the moment. See if you can get in touch with your real feelings and let them speak." The client can be encouraged to deal with any reservations about this, until some utterance is delivered. When the thoughts and feelings have been delivered in full, or as fully as is possible in the present, the coach can say: "Now imagine that you are your boss. Take a moment to get into that character, and when you are ready, talk back to the person who has just spoken."

A process like this is very possible to do on the phone, and may result in greater insight than could be achieved by any other method.

Personification in supervision

Supervision is the practice of therapists having regular meetings with senior colleagues for the purpose of discussing their work in detail. Humanistic therapists believe this practice is necessary all through their careers, not just in training, because they recognize that therapy is quite a solitary pursuit, and that there is always a danger of narcissism building up over time. Therapists who believe that they have gone beyond the necessity for regular supervision may be deceiving themselves. In the early days supervision may be mainly about technique, but in the later years it may be about the deepening of self-awareness. For the transpersonal therapist this deepening of awareness may be particularly important, and supervision may sometimes become a spiritual discipline in itself, although it is not the same as spiritual direction, which is a different discipline with a different history.

There is now a sizeable literature on supervision, some of it very good. There are courses in supervision, qualifications in supervision, accreditation in supervision. Instead of being something one "got landed with" at a senior stage in one's development as a therapist, it has become a speciality within the whole field of psychotherapy and counselling. (I shall use the word therapy to encompass both.)

The point has been made many times (Rowan 1998a, 2005b; Wilber, Engler & Brown 1986) that if we take seriously the idea that there is such a thing as psychospiritual development, then therapy can be adapted to various stages within that. If we take as our guide the Wilber (2000a) categories of Mental Ego, Centaur and Psychic/Subtle (or Subtle for short), then forms or schools of therapy turn out to be particularly suited to one or other of these levels. For example, cognitive/behavioural approaches are particularly suited to the Mental Ego level, because they both assume the same notion of the self: a role-playing self which seeks esteem from other people. Similarly, person-centred therapy, Gestalt therapy, existential analysis and psychodrama are particularly suited to the Centaur level, because they all assume the same notion of the self: an autonomous self which is deeply concerned with authenticity, spontaneity, creativity and bodymind unity. And similarly again, transpersonal psychotherapy, psychosynthesis and some of the Jungian and post-Jungian approaches are particularly suited to the Subtle level, because they all assume the same notion of the self: a self open to contact by symbols of the divine, and also open to the souls of other people. Ken Wilber (1981) was the first to be clear about these matters, but the intervening years have added a great deal of elaboration to this basic insight (see for example Wilber, Engler & Brown 1986). In recent years there has been more appreciation of the fact that therapy can also be pursued at the Causal and the Nondual levels (Almaas 1988; Prendergast, Fenner & Krystal 2003; Rowan 2005b).

	1.	**2.**	**3.**	**4.**
WILBER LEVEL	**MENTAL EGO**	**CENTAUR**	**SUBTLE**	**CAUSAL NONDUAL**
Wilber colours	Orange	Green-Teal-Turquoise	Indigo Violet	Ultraviolet-Clear Light
ROWAN POSITION	**Instrumental Self**	**Authentic Self**	**Transpersonal Self 1 (Soul)**	**Transpersonal Self 2 (Spirit)**
WADE LEVEL	**Egocentric Conformist Achievement Affiliative**	**Authentic**	**Transcendent**	**Unity**
Definition	I am defined by others	I define who I am	I am defined by the Other(s)	I am not defined
Motivation	Need	Choice	Allowing	Surrender
Personal goal	Adjustment	Self-actualization	Contacting	Union
Social goal	Socialization	Liberation	Extending	Salvation
Process	Healing – Ego-Building	Development – Ego-Extending	Opening – Ego-Reduction	Enlightenment
Buddhism	Nirmanakaya	Nirmanakaya	Sambhogakaya	Dharmakaya
Great exemplar	Albert Ellis	James Bugental	Roberto Assagioli	Shankara
Ego	Dominant	Transformed	Light	Open
Story example	Erickson	May or Wheelis	Naropa	George Fox
Traditional role of helper	Physician Analyst	Growth Facilitator	Advanced Guide	Priest(ess) Sage
Representative approaches	Hospital treatment Chemotherapy Some psy-ana Directive Behaviour mod Cognitive-behavioural Some TA Crisis work REBT Brief therapy Solution based Cognitive	Primal Integration Gestalt therapy Some psy-ana Psychodrama Open encounter Bodywork therapies Some TA Person-centred Co-counselling Regression Experiential Existential	Psycho-synthesis Some Jungians Some pagans Transpersonal Voice Dialogue Some Wicca or Magic Kabbalah Some astrology Some Tantra Shamanism Core process Holotropic	Mystical Buddhism Raja Yoga Taoism Monasticism Da Avabhasa Christian mysticism Sufi Goddess mystics Some Judaism Advaita Impersonal Buddha

continues

Figure 7 Four positions in personal development.

	1.	**2.**	**3.**	**4.**
WILBER LEVEL	**MENTAL EGO**	**CENTAUR**	**SUBTLE**	**CAUSAL**
ROWAN POSITION	Instrumental Self	Authentic Self	Transpersonal Self 1 (Soul)	Transpersonal Self 2 (Spirit)
WADE LEVEL	Egocentric Achievement Affiliative	Authentic	Transcendent	Unity
Focus	Individual and Group	Group and Individual	Supportive Community	Ideal Community
Representative names	Freud Ellis LeBon Beck Eysenck Skinner Lazarus Watzlawick Marinoff Haley Erickson Linehan Ivey Egan NLP Dryden Rangell	Maslow Rogers Mahrer Perls Searles Laing Moreno Winnicott Lomas Bugental Hycner Bohart Satir Bozarth Spinelli van Deurzen Rollo May	Jung Hillman Starhawk Assagioli Gordon-Brown Mary Watkins Jean Houston Bolen Stan Grof Boorstein Whitmore Nathan Field Fukuyama Maguire Milner Eigen Henri Corbin	Eckhart Prendergast Peter Fenner Mark Epstein Rosenbaum Ram Dass A H Almaas Sheila Krystal George Fox David Brazier Bryan Wittine Amy Mindell Adyashantii Bradford Suzuki Welwood Horne
Intuition	Chancy	Reliable	Constant	Not needed
Compassion	Subject to fatigue	Reliable	Juicy	Constant Steady
Research methods	Qualitative Quantitative	Collaborative Action research	Transformative Mindful	None
Questions	What is the best method?	What is the best relationship?	How far can we go together?	Dare you face the loss of all your words?
Questions	Dare you face the challenge of unconscious?	Dare you face the challenge of freedom?	Dare you face the loss of your boundaries?	Dare you face the loss of all your symbols?
Key issues	Acceptability Respect	Autonomy Authenticity	Openness Vision	Devotion Commitment

Figure 7 (continued)

I want to look at each of the levels mentioned in relation to personification, and make some points about the integration of all this.

Mental Ego

The general description of the Mental Ego level may be found in the work
of Ken Wilber, and I have summarized the relevant parts of the model in
my book on the transpersonal (Rowan 2005a). Figure 7 summarises the
position sufficiently for this chapter.

The supervisee at this level is seen as a learner technician, who has to be
helped to improve the technique. I have seen little evidence that the
technique of personification is used much at this level. This perhaps because
it brings the therapist into such a close relationship with the client that it
perhaps goes against the objectivity which is sought at this level

Real self or Centaur

The general description of this level of work is to be found in my book on
the subject, *The Reality Game* (Rowan 1998b). See the summary in column
two of Figure 7. It is usually described as the humanistic type of work,
although recently Leslie Greenberg and others have sometimes used the
term "experiential" instead of "humanistic" (see Greenberg, Watson &
Lietaer 1998).

Here the goal is seen, certainly by Ernst Beier and David Young, as
helping the supervisee in the work of encouraging the client to question and
vary his routines and accept the uncertainty which is a by-product of
interpersonal exploration (Beier & Young 1980, p.196). Freedom to explore
is regarded as important. Questioning rather than acceptance is what is
asked of the supervisee. Confrontation may become very important if the
supervisee becomes too passive or uncreative.

Creativity, or the ability to make effective personal changes, is regarded
as very important, and can be seen as starting with this freedom to explore.
Spontaneity is regarded as important both in the supervision and in the
therapeutic work itself, and this is strongly encouraged. The vision of the
supervisee is regarded as very important.

There is a continual questioning of narrowness. The body is included; the
social system is included; the family of origin is included; traumatic
experience is included; different kinds of relationship are included. It is
regarded as important not to leave things out. There is an experiential and
holistic approach all the time.

Above all, it is said by Peter Hawkins and Robin Shohet, supervision is a
place where both parties are constantly learning and to stay a good
supervisor is to return to question, not only the work of the supervisee, but

also what you yourself do as supervisor and how you do it (Hawkins & Shohet 2000, Chap. 4). Gaie Houston asks the question: Is the supervisor taking the supervisee forward at the right pace toward self-confidence based on reality, and toward abundance motivation? (See Houston 1995, p.95.)

Supervision is often seen as a containing and enabling process, rather than an educational or therapeutic process. According to Steve Page and Val Wosket, supervision, to be effective, must be exploratory (Page & Wosket 1994, p.39). This is because it is believed, as Laura Rice tells us, that for both supervisor and supervisee there is the basic growth motivation, a push toward differentiation, authenticity and new experience (Rice 1980, p.138). The growth and development of the supervisee is most important. Gary Yontef has drawn attention to the use of role playing in supervision, saying that "Role playing is frequently used in individual and group supervision and can be very effective. The supervisee can play the patient . . ." (Yontef 1997, p.158). This use of personification is very conducive to the uncovering of new insights, and Yontef goes on to say that this kind of personification "enables supervisees to experiment with new approaches and experience how they feel . . ."

What is regarded as central is not education or correction or monitoring but, as Margaret Rioch and her colleagues used to insist, increased self-awareness both for supervisor and supervisee (Rioch, Coulter & Weinberger 1976, p.3). There is little emphasis on correct technique, or the precision of one theory. It is more important for supervisor and supervisee both to be fully present in the supervision session, which will help to enable the therapist to be fully present with the client in the therapy session. There is often an emphasis on integration and/or eclecticism. Often the question of aims is deliberately disregarded or deemphasized; in any case aims tend to be long-term rather than short-term.

Simplicity is encouraged. The main focus is on the supervisee rather than on the client. A peer relationship is aimed at, as the ultimate goal. Jill Freedman and Gene Combs visited the Milan School, and found that supervision of family therapy, using a one-way mirror, involved a group of supervisees behind the screen engaging in real discussions of what could be done. "Although the goal of these discussions was to arrive at a single intervention or message, the oft-repeated slogan, 'Flirt with your hypotheses, but don't marry them' suggested that this goal was not in any way held to be the singular or final truth" (Freedman & Combs 1996, p.7).

The supervisee may take on the role of the client, and go back and forth between "therapist" and "client" until something illuminating emerges. This is obviously a use of the basic idea of the dialogical self, elaborated into the use of personification. Gary Yontef has noted that in Gestalt supervision role playing is frequently used in individual and group supervision and can be very effective. "The supervisee can play the patient, and the supervisor or another group member can be therapist. Various forms of role reversal can be used" (Yontef 1997, p.158). Many more ideas like this are to be found in Houston (1995). And Hawkins and Shohet (2000) point out that this can be very useful in the exploration of countertransference (p.79).

There is often a real concern for the social and political implications of the work, and both the therapist and the client may be encouraged to take action in the direction of liberation, particularly in the case of oppressive regimes. The supervisor may draw attention to the need for more heed to be paid to the social/political/economic context.

Subtle self or Transpersonal 1

The general description of this level of work is to be found in my own book on the subject (Rowan 2005a), and William West has also written well about it. Also included is what is sometimes referred to as psychospiritual therapy (West 2000), though I prefer the term transpersonal. This clarifies the basic distinctions which outline the field. Wilber (1981) is also useful. See column three of Figure 7 for a summary.

So far as supervision is concerned, there is a lot of emphasis on the further development of the supervisee, and on the enlargement of the supervisee. There is an encouragement of the subtle perception and intuition of the supervisee. Joe Henderson says the supervisee may need further education in the whole field of mythology and of archetypes, as part of the work of developing the ability to use the superconscious in therapy. The term "soul" may be used (Henderson 1995, p.156).

It could also be said at this level, as Valerie James suggests, that the supervisory situation is a *temenos*, a sacred space within which transformation may take place. The supervisor is responsible for the integrity of the container within which the therapist may be transformed (James 1996). The supervisor, like the therapist, is a wounded healer.

The whole interaction may be seen in archetypal terms. At any one moment of time, as Petruska Clarkson has suggested, any supervisor may need to be a Cerberus guarding the territories and boundaries, or a Psyche-sorter of the wheat and barley of primary and secondary realities, or a Zeus-like referee between warring internal or external factions, or a Chironic mentor teaching and modelling the skills of healing, or even a Hestian flame of spiritual direction (Clarkson 1998, p.143). John Beebe feels that the trickster archetype may certainly become involved in the double existence of the therapist being healer and healed at the same time (Beebe 1995, p.103).

Crittenden Brookes has pointed out that the supervisor may need to encourage the therapist to educate the client in confronting the numinous and archetypal layers of their own experience (Brookes 1995, p.122). Lionel Corbett suggests that numinosity, like transference, may not be noticed until it is drawn to the therapist's attention (Corbett 1995, p.75). Also it may be noted, as Noel Cobb has critically suggested, that many schools of therapy teach therapists how to run sessions with clients in such a way that they actually prevent any incursion of the sublime (Cobb 1997, p.275).

From this point of view, instead of a focus exclusively on the personalistic aspects of the transference, the supervisor would also be interested in its archetypal aspects. As Lionel Corbett says, there is a deep interest in how the Self manifests itself in the therapeutic field (Corbett 1995, p.70). As we have seen an archetype may be taken as an I-position in therapy, and it is equally possible to let this happen in supervision.

Or supervision may be seen in shamanic terms. Some supervisors, such as David Henderson, believe that the Shaman is the original expression of the archetypal intent in human society, but that over time some aspects of the Shaman's identity have split off and developed a character and autonomy of their own (Henderson 1998, p.65).

From this kind of imaginal perspective, the significance of fantasy is discovered not so much through analyzing or unmasking it, as through elaboration and following its lead. In other words, as David Maclagan has suggested, fantasy is treated less as an object of suspicion, and more as a resource to be tapped. And this is true whether we are talking about individual or group therapy (Maclagan 1997, p.63). Personification is one form of imagery, after all.

Analysis may be regarded as a mysticism of persons – and hence polyvalent, pluralistic, many-headed, many-bodied. As Andrew Samuels has insisted, the "Mundus Imaginalis" is given due weight in the thinking of both supervisor and supervisee. This is the imaginal world so well described by the Sufi scholar Henry Corbin (Samuels 1997, pp.158–164). In this case supervision too would partake of this character. It would involve the superconscious. At this level intuition ceases to be a chancy thing, and starts to become the basic way in which one thinks. It would involve a regular opening up to contact with the divine, the sacred. As Joe Henderson has told us, this may then be experienced as an initiation (Henderson 1995, pp.157–158).

There may well be an interest in the social and political context, as Samuels (1993) has suggested, and here the concern tends to be towards the long-term good, rather than towards briefer campaigns.

You could say that when the therapist comes for supervision, he or she is going on retreat. They come to stop and listen, to open their awareness. Diana Whitmore has told us that the supervisor is providing the space for retreat, the holding for retreat and the transpersonal context for retreat (Whitmore 1999, p.3).

It is sometimes felt, certainly by Diana Whitmore in the psychosynthesis tradition, that supervision from a transpersonal context requires an act of will on the part of the supervisor, to affirm that all supervision begins with the supervisor's internal state of consciousness and a commitment to work from the "inside out" before even meeting the supervisee. This is a contrary attitude to "outside in", where the supervisor is regarded as the expert and as doing something to the supervisee (Whitmore 1999, p.1). This would emphasize the transpersonal frame of the work as important.

Sometimes it is found, say Bonnie Rabin and Robert Walker of the Naropa Institute, that it is helpful for both supervisor and supervisee to have a personal mindfulness-awareness meditation practice, although this is not absolutely necessary (Rabin & Walker, n.d.).

An interesting new development is that people from the person-centred school have started to talk about subtle energies, and Rose Cameron in particular has had some very useful things to say about transpersonal supervision. "The counsellor's energetic state has an enormous impact on the therapeutic relationship. It is therefore important to develop energetic self-awareness: supervision is an excellent forum in which to do this" (Cameron 2004, p.180).

Intuition, which is very important in therapy at this level, is also important in supervision, and Rachel Charles has acknowledged this in her important book on intuition. "Supervisors are indeed sometimes presented with a 'hunch' or a 'gut feeling' about a client, a strong sense of something, but without the supervisee being able to clarify it, or pinpoint the origin of the impression" (Charles 2004, p.189). Here is subtle level material being properly acknowledged.

In a similar way, the late James Bugental, who bridges in a unique way the gap between the existential and the humanistic, as witness the tributes to him published in the Special Section of the *Journal of Humanistic Psychology* (Vol. 36 No. 4) in the Autumn of 1996, has introduced some research by Molly Sterling using the basic idea of personification. The supervisee role-plays the client and the supervisor role-plays the supervisee. Sometimes a curious thing happened:

> Unexpectedly and suddenly, I lose the ability to maintain the immersion I have been experiencing. The distinctions between "me" and "the role-played client" dissolve. It is as though there is a collapse of the separated consciousnesses into one *melded* experience . . . I can't tell which of us is the source of the content I am expressing!
>
> (Sterling & Bugental 1993, p.42)

Bugental speculates that if our deepest nature is manifested by the meld, we may arrive at a rather different picture of our own nature. He goes on into some transpersonal thoughts. So in supervision the phenomenon which is generally called "linking" (Rowan 2005a, Chap. 6) can indeed emerge, and I would argue that linking is always a subtle phenomenon.

The Causal self or Transpersonal 2

It is also possible to do supervision at the causal level, although this is much less common and hardly written about anywhere. But if it is possible to work in therapy at the causal stage (Rowan 2005c) then it must be possible to do supervision at that level also. What is the difference between the subtle and the causal? Briefly, the Subtle level is the realms of symbols and images, while at the Causal level there are no symbols or images. It would be inappropriate, therefore, to try to use personification in this level of work.

Crosscultural work

It has been pointed out that there is a particular role for the transpersonal therapist in the field of crosscultural work, because of the increased respect for all religious experiences which comes with transpersonal development. The research paper by Cinnirella and Loewenthal (1999), for example, shows that members of communities such as White Christian, Pakistani Muslim, Indian Hindu, Orthodox Jewish and Afro-Caribbean Christian have many different attitudes to counselling and psychotherapy. Some of these make them particularly suspicious of Western types of therapy. It is the transpersonal approach (not mentioned in that paper) which would be the most likely bridge for such people to use, in order to get the benefit of adequate therapy. The supervisor's role in this can be to encourage the transpersonal therapist to look for such experience and to make his or her presence known to the relevant people. Not quite in the same category, but offering the same kind of disconcerting experiences, is the multicultural work involving discarnate entities of one kind and another, ranging from gods and goddesses to demons and devils, and from loas, orishas and zar to ghosts and witches. A great deal of fear may be aroused by such material for the client, and may be picked up by a therapist who is not well versed in this area. The excellent book of Fukuyama and Sevig (1999) can be very helpful in such cases. The transpersonal therapist is of course much better able to handle this material than other therapists, because their experience of the Psychic and the Subtle realms, and the transformations of consciousness, will stand them in good stead (see Wilber et al. 1986). Also the whole idea of the pre/trans fallacy may be important, in placing the phenomenon into the right place. Again the work of the supervisor may be much needed here. Indeed, the supervisor may get out of their depth too, and have to refer to a specialist. But the simple fact of having been opened up to that level of spiritual reality may well be enough to deal with most problems. Personification can be very useful here. As Barbara Ingram points out, "a person going through the process of acculturation could be asked to dialogue with the 'Native Land Self' and the 'New Home Self'" (Ingram 2006, p.368).

As always with this kind of model, it seems worthwhile to utter the caveat that we cannot jump levels at will. We cannot will ourselves into the second column unless and until we have done the work on ourselves which can take us there. We cannot become transpersonal supervisors without doing the transpersonal work on ourselves. It is, however, possible to access all of these states temporarily, for a visit, so to speak. The rubric here is: "States are free, stages have to be earned." There are some huge challenges here, as well as some amazing opportunities.

New directions

In concluding it will be useful to have a look at the final speech of the 2008 conference, coming from Hubert Hermans. One of the most important points he made was that the theory of the dialogical self offers a fourth position on the self, in the following way.

Our traditional view used to be that the self was defined by a meaningful hierarchical cosmic order. In other words, we all believed in God, and that this meant a connectedness to the source of all goodness and truth. It also means that we used to see a distinction between mere living on earth and a destiny which involved a higher, better kind of life in Heaven. But one of the key things which went with this way of seeing the world and the self was that the cosmic order gave us a responsibility to lead a moral life. And this idea of moral responsibility went with the knowledge of how to lead a good life in accordance with the cosmic order. To be moral was to be in line with the Universe.

This notion was succeeded historically by the view of life which is often called the modern. Here we find self-contained individualism. No longer are we identified in a deep way with the cosmos – in fact we have no complicity in language, culture and community, but are quite independent. The self is its own ground, and has its own agency. We are all responsible for ourselves, and only for ourselves.

After many years of this, there began a postmodern revolution, whereby the self became decentred. Instead of a single agency, with choice and central responsibility, we got multiplicity, fragmentation and loss of agency. The self was nothing more than a linguistic construction. Power relations took the place of socially constructed roles, fixed and honoured by all. Fragmentation took another turn, and became the rule in every sphere.

But now we have, in the notion of the dialogical self, a way of keeping all these versions alive in a different way, such that they can all live together. Through the lens of the dialogical self, we can acknowledge the existence of power relations as very important indeed; we can also support a very real agency for each human being; and the idea of moral responsibility comes back as an important concept: we are responsible for ourselves and there is such a thing as a moral order – both within the person as a coherence and a realization, and outside the person as a social reality.

Some of this thinking was foreshadowed by writers in the book based on the third international conference on the dialogical self, held in Warsaw. It is edited by Piotr Oles and Hubert Hermans (2005), and represents the latest attempt to bring together the new material on the dialogical self – the theory which promises to link most of the known forms of therapy and personality theory into a single framework.

After a strong introduction by the editors, the first chapter is by Vincent Hevern, who writes about dialogical selves in the human digital ecology. He says, among other things, that

> Hermans (2003) summarises the characteristics of the dialogical self as an "embodied, spatialized, extended, socialized and open system with dialogical relations" (p.109) between "a dynamic multiplicity of relatively autonomous I-positions in an imaginal landscape" (Hermans 1996, p.33). As these remarks should make clear, I believe that the formulation of Hermans and his colleagues about how selves function in the contemporary world finds a major instantiation in the activity of individuals online. Within the human digital ecology, the dialogical self acts in ways fully consistent with and expressive of this understanding.
>
> (Hevern 2005, p.20)

This brings the dialogical self into the expanded openness of cyberspace. And in the next chapter, Colin Grant writes about information overload, globalization and the risks of the dialogical self.

Without going too deeply into the rest of the book, it can be seen that the notion of the dialogical self is taking a new turn towards a global dimension. What we have here is an integrative view of the self which does much better justice to what is going on today. Coming back to the book, Chapter 8, by Claire Haggard, opens up a discussion of the "unfinalizable self" – the self which as critically described by researchers such as Leder (1990), Burkitt (1999) and Merleau-Ponty (1968) leads us to "assume the uncomfortable and thus decentralized position of acknowledging that there can be no one single definition or theory or self" (p.119).

This is a very important insight, which delivers us from the awful responsibility of claiming the last word on the self.

What is so interesting about this book is the variety of origins of all these writers. They come from the Netherlands, Canada, Poland, Portugal, Brazil, England, South Africa, the United States, Italy and Scotland. It is clear that the dialogical self is a notion that is becoming quite widespread. At the fifth international conference in 2008 there was representation from 45 countries, and the next book will have to be much larger.

More recently, Hermans has been writing about globalization, and the idea of the dialogical self has really taken off. In a recent article he says he "aims to present a dialogical framework that serves as a link between the historical and social phenomenon of globalization on the one hand and the biologically rooted needs for stability and security on the other hand" (Hermans & Dimaggio 2007, p.32).

This whole book is an exploration of the new approach of the dialogical self, showing how it can be used in psychotherapy and counselling, and discovering its relation to all that has gone before. I hope it will be found useful. In particular, it shows how the powerful idea of the dialogical self actually reinforces the most recent ideas on the relationship, and makes a most interesting way of relating many different therapies one to another.

Bibliography

Allison, R. & Schwartz, T. (1980) *Minds in Many Pieces*, New York: Rawson-Wade.

Almaas, A. H. (1988) *The Pearl Beyond Price: Integration of personality into being: An object relations approach*, Berkeley, CA: Diamond Books.

Angus, L. & McLeod, J. (eds) (2004) *The Handbook of Narrative and Psychotherapy: Practice, theory and research*, London: Sage.

Assagioli, R. (1975) *Psychosynthesis*, London: Turnstone.

Avants, S. K. & Margolin, A. (2004) "Development of spiritual self-schema (3-S) therapy for the treatment of addictive and HIV risk behavior: A convergence of cognitive and Buddhist psychology", *Journal of Psychotherapy Integration*, 14/3, 253–289.

Baerveldt, C. & Voestermans, P. (1996) "The body as a selfing device", *Theory and Psychology*, 6/4, 693–713.

Bakhtin, M. M. (1973) *Problems of Dostoevsky's Poetics* (2nd ed.) (trans. R. W. Rotsel), Ann Arbor, MI: Ardis. (First ed. published in 1929 under the title *Problemy tvorchestva Dostoevskogo*.)

Bakhtin, M. M. (1981) *The Dialogic Imagination: Four essays*, Austin, TX: University of Texas Press.

Balint, M. (1968) *The Basic Fault*, London: Tavistock.

Bandler, J. & Grinder, R. (1982) *Reframing*, Moab, UT: Real People Press.

Baumgartner, P. & Perls F. S. (1975) *Gifts from Lake Cowichan and Legacy from Fritz*, Palo Alto, CA: Science & Behaviour Books Inc.

Beahrs, J. O. (1982) *Unity and Multiplicity*, New York: Brunner/Mazel.

Beebe, J. (1995) "Sustaining the potential analyst's morale", in P. Kugler (ed) *Jungian Perspectives on Clinical Supervision*, Einsiedeln, Switzerland: Daimon.

Beier, E. G. & Young, D. M. (1980) "Supervision in communications analytic therapy", in A. K. Hess (ed) *Psychotherapy Supervision: Theory, research and practice*, New York: John Wiley.

Beisser, A. (1972) "The paradoxical theory of change", in J. Fagan & I. L. Shepherd (eds) *Gestalt Therapy Now*, New York: Harper.

Berne, E. (1961) *Transactional Analysis in Psychotherapy*, London: Evergreen Books.

Berne, E. (1972) *What Do You Say After You Say Hello?*, New York: Grove Press.

Biechonski, J. (2007a) *Myths, Dreams and Fairy Tales* (DVD), SACH International, www.sachinternational.com.

Biechonski, J. (2007b) *Psycho-Neuro-Immunology* (DVD), SACH International, www.sachinternational.com.

Binet, A. (1892) *Les alterations de la personnalité*, Paris: Alcan.

Boa, F. (1988) *The Way of the Dream*, Toronto: Windrose Films.

Blatner, H. (1970) "Psychodrama, role-playing and action methods: Theory and practice", Mimeographed.

Bogart, V. (1994) "Transcending the dichotomy of either 'subpersonalities' or 'an integrated unitary self'", *Journal of Humanistic Psychology*, 34/2, 82–89.

Bogart, V. (2007) *Explore the Undiscovered You: Three paths to self-discovery and empowerment*, Walnut Creek, CA: Baskin Publishing.

Bolen, J. S. (1984) *Goddesses in Everywoman*, New York: Harper & Row.

Braten, S. (1992) "The virtual other in infants' minds and social feeling", in A. H. Wold (ed) *The Dialogical Alternative*, Oxford: Oxford University Press.

Bromberg, P. M. (1998) *Standing in the Spaces: Essays in clinical process, trauma and dissociation*, London: The Analytic Press.

Bromberg, P. M. (2004) "Standing in the spaces: The multiplicity of self and the psychoanalytic relationship", in H. J. M. Hermans & G. Dimaggio (eds) *The Dialogical Self in Therapy*, London: Brunner-Routledge.

Brookes, C. E. (1995) "On supervision in Jungian continuous case seminars", in P. Kugler (ed) *Jungian Perspectives on Clinical Supervision*, Einsiedeln, Switzerland: Daimon.

Brown, M. Y. (1993) *Growing Whole: Self-realization on an endangered planet*, Center City, MN: Hazelden.

Brown, M. Y. (2004) *Unfolding Self: The practice of psychosynthesis*, New York: Helios Press.

Bruner, J. (1986) *Actual Minds, Possible Worlds*, Cambridge, MA: Harvard University Press.

Bruner, J. (1990) *Acts of Meaning*, Cambridge, MA: Harvard University Press.

Burkitt, I. (1999) *Bodies of Thought: Embodiment, identity and modernity*, London: Sage.

Cameron, R. (2004) "Shaking the spirit: Subtle energy awareness in supervision", in K. Tudor & M. Worrall (eds) *Freedom to Practise: Person-centred approaches to supervision*, Ross-on-Wye, UK: PCCS Books.

Carlson, E. T. (1986) "The history of dissociation until 1880", in J. M. Quen (ed) *Split Minds/Split Brain*, New York & London: New York University Press.

Chamberlain, D. (1998) *The Mind of Your Newborn Baby*, Berkeley, CA: North Atlantic Books.

Charles, R. (2004) *Intuition in Psychotherapy and Counselling*, London: Whurr.

Chertok, L. & de Saussure, R. (1979) *The Therapeutic Revolution: From Mesmer to Freud*, New York: Brunner/Mazel.

Cinnirella, M. & Loewenthal, K. M. (1999) "Religious and ethnic group influences on beliefs about mental illness: A qualitative interview study", *British Journal of Medical Psychology*, 72/4, 505–524.

Clarkson, P. (1992) *Transactional Analysis Psychotherapy: An integrated approach*, London: Routledge.

Clarkson, P. (1995) *The Therapeutic Relationship*, London: Whurr.

Clarkson, P. (2003) *The Therapeutic Relationship* (2nd ed.), London: Whurr.

Clarkson, P. (1998) "Supervised supervision: Including the archetopoi of supervision", in P. Clarkson (ed) *Supervision: Psychoanalytic and Jungian perspectives*, London: Whurr.

Clarkson, P. & Mackewn, J. (1993) *Fritz Perls*, London: Sage.

Cobb, N. (1997) "On the sublime: Eva Loewe and the practice of psychotherapy, or Aphrodite in the consulting room", in P. Clarkson (ed) *On the Sublime in Psychoanalysis, Archetypal Psychology and Psychotherapy*, London: Whurr.

Cooper, M. & Cruthers, H. (1999) "Facilitating the expression of subpersonalities: A review and analysis of techniques", in J. Rowan & M. Cooper (eds) *The Plural Self: Multiplicity in everyday life*, London: Sage.

Corbett, L. (1995) "Supervision and the mentor archetype", in P. Kugler (ed) *Jungian Perspectives on Clinical Supervision*, Einsiedeln, Switzerland: Daimon.

Corsini, R. J. (1981) *Handbook of Innovative Psychotherapies*, New York: John Wiley.

Cortright, B. (2007) *Integral Psychology*, Albany, NY: SUNY Press.

Cronin-Lampe, K., Tufuga, P., TeKira, S. & Herbert, A. (1999) "Talking with Dak", in D. Denborough & C. White (eds) *Extending Narrative Therapy*, Adelaide, Australia: Dulwich Centre.

Danziger, K. (1997) "The varieties of social construction", *Theory and Psychology*, 7/3, 399–416.

Decker, H. H. (1986) "The lure of nonmaterialism in materialist Europe: Investigations of dissociative phenomena 1880–1915", in M. Quen (ed) *Split Minds/Split Brain*, New York & London: New York University Press.

Denzin, N. K. (1987) "A phenomenology of the emotionally divided self", in K. Yardley & T. Honess (eds) *Self and Identity*, Chichester, UK: John Wiley.

Dimaggio, G., Catania, D., Salvatore, G., Carcione, A. & Nicolo, G. (2006) "Psychotherapy of paranoid personality disorder from the perspective of dialogical self theory", *Counselling Psychology Quarterly*, 19/1, 69–87.

Dimaggio, G., Fiore, D., Salvatore, G. & Carcione, A. (2007) "Dialogical relationship patterns in narcissistic personalities: Session analysis and treatment implications", *Journal of Constructivist Psychology*, 20, 23–51.

Dunkel, C. & Kerpelman, J. (eds) (2006) *Possible Selves: Theory, research and applications*, New York: Nova Science.

Dyak, M. (1999) *The Voice Dialogue Facilitator's Handbook: Part 1*, Seattle: L.I.F.E. Energy Press.

Ecker, B. & Hulley, L. (1996) *Depth-oriented Brief Therapy*, San Francisco: Jossey-Bass.

Egan, G. (1976) "Confrontation", *Group and Organization Studies*, 1/2, 223–243.

Ellenberger, H. (1970) *The Discovery of the Unconscious*, New York: Basic Books.

Elliott, J. (1976) *The Theory and Practice of Encounter Group Leadership*, Berkeley, CA: Explorations Institute.

Elliott, R. & Greenberg, L. S. (1997) "Multiple voices in process-experiential therapy: Dialogues between aspects of the self", *Journal of Psychotherapy Integration*, 7, 225–239.

Elliott, R., Davis, K. L. & Slatick, E. (1998) "Process-experiential therapy for posttraumatic stress difficulties", in L. S. Greenberg, J. C. Watson & G. Lietaer (eds) *Handbook of experiential psychotherapy*, New York: Guilford Press.

Ernst, S. & Goodison, L. (1981) *In Our Own Hands: A book of self-help therapy*, London: The Women's Press.

Eron, J. B. & Lund, T. W. (1996) *Narrative Solutions in Brief Therapy*, New York: Guilford Press.

Faber, M. D. (1977) "Don Juan and Castaneda: The psychology of altered awareness", *The Psychoanalytic Review*, 64/3, 323–379.

Fadiman, J. (1993) "Who's minding the store? A comment on Frick's defense of unitary personality", *Journal of Humanistic Psychology*, 33/2, 129–133.

Fairbairn, W. R. D. (1952) *Psychoanalytic Studies of the Personality*, London: Tavistock.

Federn, P. (1952) *Ego Psychology and the Psychoses*, New York: Basic Books.

Fenner, P. (2007) *Radiant Mind: Awakening unconditioned awareness*, Boulder, CO: Sounds True.

Ferenczi, S. (1909) "Introjection and transference", in *First Contributions to Psychoanalysis*, London: Hogarth Press (1952).

Ferrucci, P. (1982) *What We May Be*, Wellingborough, UK: Turnstone Press.

Field, N. (1996) *Breakdown and Breakthrough*, London: Routledge.

Fogel, A., de Koeyer, I., Bellagamba, F. & Bell, H. (2002) "The dialogical self in the first two years of life", *Theory and Psychology*, 12/2, 191–205.

Fonagy, P. & Target, M. (1996) "Playing with reality I: Theory of mind and the normal development of psychic reality", *International Journal of Psychoanalysis*, 77, 217–233.

Franklin, M. (1981) "Play as the creation of imaginary situations: The role of language", in S. Wapner & B. Kaplan (eds) *Toward a Holistic Developmental Psychology*, Hillsdale, NJ: Lawrence Erlbaum.

Fransella, F. (ed) (2003) *International Handbook of Personal Construct Psychology*, Chichester, UK: John Wiley.

Freedman, J. & Combs, G. (1996) *Narrative Therapy: The social construction of preferred realities*, New York: W. W. Norton.

Freud, S. (1923) *The Ego and the Id and Other Works (CW19)*, London: Hogarth Press.

Freud, S. (1938) "Splitting of the ego in the process of defence", *Standard Edition Vol. 23*, London: Hogarth Press.

Frey-Rohn, L. (1974) *From Freud to Jung: A comparative study of the psychology of the unconscious*, New York: G. P. Putnam's Sons.

Frick, W. B. (1993) "Subpersonalities: Who conducts the orchestra?", *Journal of Humanistic Psychology*, 33/2, 122–128.

Fuhrer, U. & Josephs, I. E. (eds) (1999) *Personliche Objecte, Identitat und Entwicklung [Personal Objects, Identity and Development]*, Göttingen, Germany: Vandenhoek & Ruprecht.

Fukuyama, M. A. & Sevig, T. D. (1999) *Integrating Spirituality into Multicultural Counselling*, Thousand Oaks, CA: Sage.

Gazzaniga, M. (1985) *The Social Brain*, New York: Basic Books.

Georgaca, E. (2001) "Voices of the self in psychotherapy: A qualitative analysis", *British Journal of Medical Psychology*, 74, 223–236.

Gergen, K. J. (1972) "Multiple identity", in *Psychology Today*, 5/12.

Gergen, K. J. (1985) "The social constructivist movement in modern psychology", *American Psychologist*, 40, 266–275.

Gergen, K. J. (1997) "The place of the psyche in a constructed world", *Theory and Psychology*, 7/6, 723–746.

Gergen, M. M. & Davis, S. N. (eds) (1997) *Toward a New Psychology of Gender: A reader*, London: Routledge.

Goffman, E. (1974) *Frame Analysis*, New York: Harper & Row.

Goldfried, M. R. (1982) "On the history of therapeutic integration", *Behavior Therapy*, 13, 572–593.

Goldman, R. (2002) "The empty-chair dialogue for unfinished business", in J. C. Watson, R. N. Goldman & M. S. Warner (eds) *Client-Centered and Experiential Psychotherapy in the 21st Century: Advances in theory, research and practice* (pp.427–447), Llangarron, UK: PCCS Books.

Goolishian, H. A. & Anderson, H. (1992) "Strategy and intervention versus nonintervention: A matter of theory?", *Journal of Marital and Family Therapy*, 18, 5–15.

Graham, H. (ed) (1995) *Mary Parker Follett: Prophet of management*, Boston: Harvard Business School Press.

Greenberg, I. A. (ed) (1974) *Psychodrama: Theory and therapy*, London: Souvenir Press.

Greenberg, L. S. (2002). *Emotion-Focused Therapy: Coaching clients to work through their feelings*, Washington, DC: APA.

Greenberg, L. S., Rice, L. N. & Elliott, R. (1993) *Facilitating Emotional Change: The moment-by-moment process*, New York: Guilford Press.

Greenberg, L. S., Watson, J. C. & Lietaer, G. (1998) *Handbook of Experiential Psychotherapy*, New York: Guilford Press.

Greer, S. (1997) "Nietzsche and social construction", *Theory and Psychology*, 7/1, 83–100.

Gregg, G. S. (1991) *Self-Representation: Life narrative studies in identity and ideology*, New York: Greenwood.

Grof, S. (1979) *Realms of the Human Unconscious*, London: Souvenir Press.

Grof, S. (1992) *The Holotropic Mind*, San Francisco: Harper.

Guidano, V. F. (1991) *The Self in Process*, New York: Guilford Press.

Guidano, V. F. (1995) "Self-observation in constructivist therapy", in R. A. Neimeyer & M. J. Mahoney (eds) *Constructivism in Psychotherapy* (pp.155–168), Washington, DC: APA.

Guntrip, H. (1971) *Psychoanalytic Theory, Therapy and the Self*, New York: Basic Books.

Gurdjieff, G. (1950) *Meetings with Remarkable Men*, London: Routledge.

Hannah, B. (1981) *Encounters with the Soul: Active imagination as developed by C. G. Jung*, Boston: Sigo Press.

Hart, T. (2000) "Deep empathy", in T. Hart, P. Nelson & K. Puhakka (eds) *Transpersonal Knowing*, Albany, NY: SUNY Press.

Hawkins, P. (1988) "A phenomenological psychodrama workshop", in P. Reason (ed) *Human Inquiry in Action: Developments in new paradigm research*, London: Sage.

Hawkins, P. & Shohet, R. (2000) *Supervision in the Helping Professions* (2nd ed.), Buckingham, UK: Open University Press.

Hegel, G. W. F. (1892) *The Logic of Hegel* (trans. W. Wallace), Oxford: Clarendon Press.

Henderson, D. (1998) "Solitude and solidarity: A philosophy of supervision", in

P. Clarkson (ed) *Supervision: Psychoanalytic and Jungian perspectives*, London: Whurr.

Henderson, J. L. (1995) "Assessing progress in supervision", in P. Kugler (ed) *Jungian Perspectives on Clinical Supervision*, Einsiedeln, Switzerland: Daimon.

Herink, R. (1980) *The Psychotherapy Handbook*, New York: New American Library.

Hermans, H. J. M. (1992) "The dialogical self: One person, different stories", in A. H. Wold (ed) *The Dialogical Alternative*, Oxford: Oxford University Press.

Hermans, H. J. M. (1996) "Voicing the self: from information processing to dialogical interchange", *Psychological Bulletin*, 119, 31–50.

Hermans, H. J. M. (1999) "The polyphony of the mind: A multi-voiced and dialogical self", in J. Rowan & M. Cooper (eds) *The Plural Self: Multiplicity in everyday life*, London: Sage.

Hermans, H. J. M. (2001) "The dialogical self: Toward a theory of personal and cultural positioning", *Culture and Psychology*, 7/3, 243–281.

Hermans, H. J. M. (2002) "The dialogical self as a society of mind", *Theory and Psychology*, 12/2, 147–160.

Hermans, H. J. M. (2003) "The construction and reconstruction of a dialogical self", *Journal of Constructivist Psychology*, 16/2, 89–130.

Hermans, H. J. M. (2004) "The dialogical self: Between exchange and power", in H. J. M. Angus & J. McLeod (eds) (2004) *The Handbook of Narrative and Psychotherapy: Practice, theory and research*, London: Sage.

Hermans, H. J. M. & Dimaggio, G. (eds) (2004) *The Dialogical Self in Psychotherapy*, London: Brunner-Routledge.

Hermans, H. J. M. & Dimaggio, G. (2007) "Self, identity, and globalization in times of uncertainty: A dialogical analysis", *Review of General Psychology*, 11/1, 31–61.

Hermans, H. J. M. & Hermans-Jansen, E. (1995) *Self-Narratives: The construction of meaning in psychotherapy*, New York: Guilford Press.

Hermans, H. J. M. & Kempen, H. J. G. (1993) *The Dialogical Self: Meaning as movement*, San Diego: Academic Press.

Hermans, H. J. M. & van Loon, R. J. P. (1991) "The personal meaning of symbols", *Journal of Religion and Health*, 30, 241–261.

Hevern, V. W. (2005) "Dialogical selves in the human digital ecology", in P. K. Oles & H. J. M. Hermans (eds) *The Dialogical Self: Theory and research*, Lublin, Poland: Wydawnictwo KUL.

Hilgard, E. R. (1986) *Divided Consciousness*, New York: John Wiley.

Hillman, J. (1975) *Re-Visioning Psychology*, New York: Harper & Row.

Hillman, J. (1983) *Archetypal Psychology: A brief account*, Dallas: Spring.

Hillman, J. (1985) *Anima: An anatomy of a personified notion*, Dallas: Spring.

Holmes, P. & Karp, M. (1991) *Psychodrama: Inspiration and technique*, London: Tavistock/Routledge.

Holmes, P., Karp, M. & Watson, M. (1994) *Psychodrama since Moreno: Innovations in theory and practice*, London: Routledge.

Honos-Webb, L., Surko, M., Stiles, W. B. & Greenberg, L. (1999) "Assimilation of voices in psychotherapy: The case of Jan", *Journal of Counselling Psychology*, 46/4, 448–460.

Horowitz, M. J. (1987) *States of Mind: Configurational analysis of individual psychology (2nd ed.)*, New York: Plenum Press.

Houston, G. (1995) *Supervision and Counselling* (new revised ed.), London: Rochester Foundation.

Hoyt, M. F. (ed) (1994) *Constructive Therapies Vol. 1*, New York: Guilford Press.

Hoyt, M. F. (ed) (1996) *Constructive Therapies Vol. 2*, New York: Guilford Press.

Hunt, D. (2003) "Being intimate with what is: Healing the pain of separation", in J. J. Prendergast, P. Fenner & S. Krystel (eds) *The Sacred Mirror: Nondual wisdom and psychotherapy*, St Paul, MN: Paragon House.

Hycner, R. (1993, 1991) *Between Person and Person: Toward a dialogical psychotherapy*, Highland, NY: Gestalt Journal Press.

Ingram, B. L. (2006) *Clinical Case Formulation: Matching the integrative treatment plan to the client*, Hoboken, NJ: John Wiley.

James, V. (1996). *Supervision and the Transpersonal* (unpublished Minster Centre dissertation).

Janov, S. (1970) *The Primal Scream*, New York: Putnam.

Joachim, H. H. (1948) *Logical Studies*, Oxford: Clarendon Press.

Johnson, R. A. (1986) *Inner Work: Using dreams and active imagination for personal growth*, San Francisco: Harper & Row.

Josephs, I. E. (1998) "Constructing one's self in the city of the silent: Dialogue, symbols, and the role of 'as-if' in self development", *Human Development*, 41, 180–195.

Josephs, I. E. (2002) "The Hopi in me: The construction of a voice in the dialogical self from a cultural psychological perspective", *Theory and Psychology*, 12/2, 161–173.

Jung, C. G. (1928) "The structure of the psyche", in *Collected Works Vol. 8*, London: Routledge.

Jung, C. G. (1946) *The Psychology of the Transference*, in *Collected Works Vol. 16*, London: Routledge.

Jung, C. G. (1966) "Psychotherapy and a philosophy of life", in *Collected Works Vol. 16*, para 179, London: Routledge.

Kahn, M. (1991) *Between Therapist and Client: The new relationship*, New York: W. H. Freeman.

Karle, H. W. A. & Boys, J. H. (1987) *Hypnotherapy: A practical handbook*, London: Free Association Books.

Karp, M., Holmes, P. & Tauvon, K. B. (eds) (1998) *The Handbook of Psychodrama*, London: Routledge.

Kauffman K. & New, C. (2004) *Co-Counselling: The theory and practice of re-evaluation counselling*, Hove, UK: Brunner-Routledge.

Kelly, G. A. (1991a) *The Psychology of Personal Constructs Vol. 1: A theory of personality*, London: Routledge (original work published 1955).

Kelly, G. A. (1991b) *The Psychology of Personal Constructs Vol. 2: Clinical diagnosis and psychotherapy*, London: Routledge (original work published 1955).

Kelly, S. L. (1998) "Revisioning the mandala of consciousness", in D. Rothberg & S. Kelly (eds) *Ken Wilber in Dialogue*, Wheaton, IL: Quest.

Kihlstrom, J. F. & Cantor, N. (1984) "Mental representations of the self", in L. Berkowitz (ed) *Advances in Experimental Social Psychology 17*, New York: Academic Press.

Kirschenbaum, H. & Henderson, V. L. (1990) *The Carl Rogers Reader*, London: Constable.

Klein, M. (1948) *Contributions to Psychoanalysis*, London: Hogarth Press.

Kohlberg, L. (1981) *The Philosophy of Moral Development*, San Francisco: Harper & Row.

Kohut, H. (1971) *The Analysis of the Self*, New York: International Universities Press.

Kohut, H. (1984) *How Does Analysis Cure?*, London: University of Chicago Press.

Laborde, G. Z. (1987) *Influencing with Integrity*, Palo Alto, CA: Syntony Publishing.

Laborde, G. Z. (1988) *Fine Tune your Brain*, Palo Alto, CA: Syntony Publishing.

Laing, R. D. (1976) *The Facts of Life*, Harmondsworth, UK: Penguin.

Lake, F. (1966) *Clinical Theology*, London: Darton, Longman & Todd.

Lake, F. (1980) *Constricted Confusion*, Oxford: Clinical Theology Association.

Langs, R. (1982) *Psychotherapy: A basic text*, New York: Jason Aronson.

Leder, D. (1990) *The Absent Body*, Chicago: University of Chicago Press.

Leiman, M. & Stiles, W. B. (2001) "Dialogical sequence analysis and the Zone of Proximal Development as conceptual enhancements to the assimilation model: The case of Jan revisited", *Psychotherapy Research*, 11, 311–330.

Leitner, L. M. (2007) "Theory, technique, and person: Technical integration in experiential constructivist psychotherapy", *Journal of Psychotherapy Integration*, 17/1, 33–49.

Lewin, K. (1936) *Topological Psychology*, New York: McGraw-Hill.

Lichtenberg, P. (2000) "Creating a distinct 'I' and a distinct 'You' in contacting", *The Gestalt Journal*, 23/2.

Lichtenberg, P. (2008) "The four corners at the intersection of contacting", *International Gestalt Journal*, 31/1.

Loevinger, J. (1976) *Ego Development*, San Francisco: Jossey-Bass.

Lyra, M. C. D. P. (1999) "An excursion into the dynamics of dialogue: Elaborations upon the dialogical self", *Culture and Psychology*, 5/4, 477–489.

Lysaker, P. H. & Lysaker, J. T. (2004) "Schizophrenia as dialogue at the ends of its tether: The relationship of disruptions in identity with positive and negative symptoms", *Journal of Constructivist Psychology*, 17, 105–120.

McAdams, D. P. (1985) "The 'Imago': A key narrative component of identity", in P. Shaver (ed) *Self, Situations and Social Behaviour*, Beverly Hills, CA: Sage.

McCulloch, W. W. (1945) "A heterarchy of values determined by the topology of nervous nets", *Bulletin of Mathematical Biophysics*.

Maclagan, D. (1997) "Fantasy, play and the image in supervision", in G. Shipton (ed) *Supervision of Psychotherapy and Counselling*, Buckingham, UK: Open University Press.

McLeod, J. (1997) *Narrative and Psychotherapy*, London: Sage.

McNamee, S. (1996) "Psychotherapy as social construction", in H. Rosen & H. T. Kuehlwein (eds) *Constructing Reality: Meaning-making perspectives for psychotherapists* (pp.115–117), San Francisco: Jossey-Bass.

Mahoney, M. J. (1992) "Scientific psychology and radical behaviorism: Important distinctions based in scientism and objectivism", in R. B. Miller (ed) *The Restoration of Dialogue: Readings in the philosophy of clinical psychology*, Washington, DC: APA.

Mahoney, M. J. (2003) *Constructive Psychotherapy*, New York: Guilford Press.

Mahrer, A. R. (1978) *Experiencing*, New York: Brunner/Mazel.

Mahrer, A. R. (1983) *Experiential Psychotherapy*, New York: Brunner/Mazel.

Mahrer, A. R. (1986) *Therapeutic Experiencing*, New York: W. W. Norton.

Mair, M. (1977) "The community of self", in D. Bannister (ed) *New Perspectives in Personal Construct Theory*, London: Academic Press.

Markus, H. & Nurius, P. (1987) "Possible selves: The interface between motivation and the self-concept", in Yardley, K. & Honess, T. (eds) *Self and Identity: Psychosocial perspectives*, Chichester, UK: John Wiley.

Martindale, C. (1980) "Subselves: The internal representation of situational and personal dispositions", in L. Wheeler (ed) *Review of Personality and Social Psychology 1*, Beverly Hills, CA: Sage.

Maslow, A. H. (1987) *Motivation and Personality* (3rd ed.), New York: Harper & Row.

May, R. (1983) *The Discovery of Being*, New York: W. W. Norton.

Mead, G. H. (1934) *Mind, Self and Society*, Chicago: University of Chicago Press.

Mearns, D. & Thorne, B. (2000) *Person-Centred Therapy Today: New frontiers in theory and practice*, London: Sage.

Mearns, D. & Cooper, M. (2005) *Working at Relational Depth in Counselling and Psychotherapy*, London: Sage.

Meichenbaum, D. (1977) *Cognitive-Behaviour Modification: An integrative approach*, New York: Plenum Press.

Merleau-Ponty, M. (1968) "The visible and the invisible", in C. Lefort (ed) *The Visible and Invisible*, Evanston, IL: Northwestern University Press.

Merzel, D. G. (2003) *The Path of the Human Being: Zen teachings on the Bodhisattva way*, Boston: Shambhala.

Middlebrook, P. N. (1974) *Social Psychology and Modern Life*, New York: Alfred A. Knopf.

Minsky, M. (1988) *The Society of Mind*, London: Picador.

Mintz, E. E. (1983) *The Psychic Thread: Paranormal and transpersonal aspects of psychotherapy*, New York: Human Sciences Press.

Moreno, Z., Blomkvist, L. D. & Rützel, T. (2000) *Psychodrama, Surplus Reality and the Art of Healing*, London: Routledge.

Mushatt, C. (1975) "Mind-Body-Environment: Toward understanding the impact of loss on psyche and soma", *Psychoanalytic Quarterly*, 44, 93.

Neimeyer, R. A. (1986) "Personal construct therapy", in W. Dryden & W. Golden (eds) *Cognitive-Behavioural Approaches to Psychotherapy*, London: Harper & Row.

Neimeyer, R. A. (2000). "Narrative disruptions in the construction of the self", in R. A. Neimeyer & J. D. Raskin (eds) *Constructions of Disorder* (pp.207–241), Washington, DC: APA.

Neimeyer, R. A. (2004) "Fostering posttraumatic growth: A narrative contribution", *Psychological Inquiry*, 15, 53–59.

Neimeyer, R. A. (2006) "Narrating the dialogical self: Toward an expanded toolbox for the counselling psychologist", *Counselling Psychology Quarterly*, 19/1, 105–120.

Neimeyer, R. A. (2009) *Constructivist Psychotherapy*, London: Routledge.

Neimeyer, R. A. & Mahoney, M. J. (eds) (1995) *Constructivism in Psychotherapy*, Washington, DC: APA.

Neimeyer, R. A. & Raskin, J. D. (eds) (2000) *Constructions of Disorder: Meaning-making frameworks for psychotherapy*, Washington, DC: APA.

Nietzsche, F. (1967/1901) *The Will to Power*, New York: Random House.

O'Connor, E. (1971) *Our Many Selves*, New York: Harper & Row.

Ogilvy, J. (1977) *Many Dimensional Man*, New York: Oxford University Press.

Oles, P. K. & Hermans, H. J. M. (2005) *The Dialogical Self: Theory and research*, Lublin, Poland: Wydawnictwo KUL.

Ornstein, R. (1986) *MultiMinds: A new way to look at human behaviour*, Boston: Houghton Mifflin.

Osatuke, K., Humphreys, C. L., Glick, M. J., Graff-Reed, R. L., Mack, L. M. & Stiles, W. B. (2005) "Vocal manifestations of internal multiplicity: Mary's voices", *Psychology and Psychotherapy: Theory, Research and Practice*, 78/1, 21–44.

Osatuke, K. & Stiles, W. B. (2006) "Problematic internal voices in clients with borderline features: an elaboration of the assimilation model", *Journal of Constructivist Psychology*, 19, 287–319.

Page, S. & Wosket, V. (1994) *Supervising the Counsellor: A cyclical model*, London: Routledge.

Parfitt, W. (1990) *Walking through Walls: Practical esoteric psychology*, Shaftesbury, UK: Element.

Perls, F. S. (1951) *Gestalt Therapy*, New York: Dell.

Perls, F. S. (1969) *Gestalt Therapy Verbatim*, Moab, UT: Real People Press.

Perls, F. S. (1976) *Eyewitness to Therapy*, New York: Bantam.

Pitzele, P. (1991) "Adolescents inside out: Intrapsychic psychodrama", in P. Holmes & M. Karp (eds) *Psychodrama: Inspiration and technique*, London: Routledge.

Prendergast, J. J., Fenner, P. & Krystal, S. (eds) (2003) *The Sacred Mirror: Nondual wisdom and psychotherapy*, St Paul, MN: Paragon House.

Prendergast, J. J. & Bradford, G. K. (eds) (2007) *Listening from the Heart of Silence (Nondual Wisdom and Psychotherapy Vol. 2)*, St Paul, MN: Paragon House.

Rabin, B. & Walker, R. (undated, 9 pages) "A contemplative approach to clinical supervision", Naropa Institute, Boulder, CO, USA.

Raskin, J. D. (2007) "Assimilative integration in constructivist psychotherapy" *Journal of Psychotherapy Integration*, 17/1, 50–69.

Raskin, J. D. & Bridges, S. K. (eds) (2002) *Studies in Meaning 1: Exploring constructivist psychology*, New York: Pace University Press.

Raskin, J. D. & Bridges, S. K. (eds) (2004) *Studies in Meaning 2: Bridging the personal and social in constructivist psychology*, New York: Pace University Press.

Redfearn, J. W. T. (1985) *My self, My Many Selves*, London: Academic Press.

Rice, L. N. (1980) "A client-centred approach to the supervision of psychotherapy", in A. K. Hess (ed) *Psychotherapy Supervision: Theory, research and practice*, New York: John Wiley.

Riegel, K. F. (1984) Chapter in M. L. Commons, F. A. Richards & C. Armon (eds) *Beyond Formal Operations: Late adolescence and adult development*, New York: Praeger.

Ring, K. (1984) *Heading Toward Omega*, New York: William Morrow.

Rioch, M. J., Coulter, W. R. & Weinberger, D. M. (1976) *Dialogues for Therapists*, San Francisco: Jossey-Bass.

Rogers, T. B. (1981) "A model of the self as an aspect of the human information processing system", in N. Cantor & J. F. Kihlstrom (eds) *Personality, Cognition and Social Interaction*, Hillsdale, NJ: Lawrence Erlbaum.

Rommetveit, R. (1992) "Outline of a dialogically-based social-cognitive approach to human cognition and communication", in A. H. Wold (ed) *The Dialogical Alternative*, Oxford: Oxford University Press.

Rowan, J. (1990) *Subpersonalities: The people inside us*, London: Routledge.

Rowan, J. (1997) *Healing the Male Psyche: Therapy as initiation*, London: Routledge.

Rowan, J. (1998a) "Transformational research", in P. Clarkson (ed) *Counselling Psychology: Integrating theory, research and supervised practice*, London: Routledge.

Rowan, J. (1998b) *The Reality Game* (2nd ed.), London: Routledge.

Rowan, J. (2001) *Ordinary Ecstasy: The dialectics of humanistic psychology* (3rd ed.), London: Brunner-Routledge.

Rowan, J. (2005a) *The Transpersonal: Spirituality in psychotherapy and counselling* (2nd ed.), London: Routledge.

Rowan, J. (2005b) "Integral psychotherapy", in J. Drew & D. Lorimer (eds) *Ways Through the Wall: Approaches to citizenship in an interconnected world*, Lydney, UK: First Stone.

Rowan, J. (2005c) "Is it possible to work at the causal level in therapy?", *Transpersonal Psychology Review*, 9/1, 41–49.

Rowan, J. & Cooper, M. (1999) *The Plural Self: Multiplicity in everyday life*, London: Sage.

Ryle, A. & Kerr, I. (2002). *Introducing Cognitive Analytic Therapy: Principles and practice*, Chichester, UK: John Wiley.

Samuels, A. (1989) *The Plural Psyche*, London, Routledge.

Samuels, A. (1993) *The Political Psyche*, London: Routledge.

Samuels, A. (1997) "Countertransference, the imaginal world and the politics of the sublime", in P. Clarkson (ed) *On the Sublime: In psychoanalysis, archetypal psychology and psychotherapy*, London: Whurr.

Samuels, A., Shorter, B. & Plaut, F. (1986) *A Critical Dictionary of Jungian Analysis*, London: Routledge & Kegan Paul.

Sarbin, T. R. (1986) "The narrative as a root metaphor for psychology", in T. R. Sarbin (ed) *Narrative Psychology: The storied nature of human conduct* (pp.1–27), New York: Praeger.

Satir, V. (1978) *Your Many Faces*, Berkeley, CA: Celestial Arts.

Satir, V. & Baldwin, M. (1983) *Satir Step by Step*, Palo Alto, CA: Science & Behavior.

Schutz, W. C. (1981) "Holistic education", in R. J. Corsini (ed) *Handbook of Innovative Psychotherapies*, New York: John Wiley.

Searles, H. F. (1986) *My Work with Borderline Patients*, Northvale, NJ: Jason Aronson.

Semerari, A., Carcione, A., Dimaggio, G., Falcone, M., Nicolò, G., Procacci, M. & Alleva, G. (2003) "How to evaluate metacognitive funtioning in psychotherapy: The Metacognition Assessment Scale and its applications", *Clinical Psychology and Psychotherapy*, 10, 238–261.

Shaffer, J. & Galinsky, M. D. (1989) *Models of Group Therapy* (2nd ed.), Englewood Cliffs, NJ: Prentice Hall.

Shapiro, S. B. (1962) "A theory of ego pathology and ego therapy", *Journal of Psychology*, 53.

Shapiro, S. B. (1976) *The Selves Inside You*, Berkeley, CA: Explorations Institute.

Shorr, J. E. (1983) *Psychotherapy Through Imagery* (2nd ed.), New York: Thieme-Stratton.

Shotter, J. (1999) "Life inside dialogically structured mentalities: Bakhtin's and Voloshinov's account of our mental activities as out in the world between us", in J. Rowan & M. Cooper (eds) *The Plural Self: Multiplicity in everyday life*, London: Sage.

Sliker, G. (1992) *Multiple Mind*, Boston: Shambhala.

Smith, P. B. (1973) *Groups Within Organizations*, London: Harper & Row.

Sperber, D. (ed) (2000). *Metarepresentation*, Oxford: Oxford University Press.

Starhawk (1987) *Truth or Dare: Encounters with power, authority and mystery*, San Francisco: Harper & Row.

Stenner, P. & Eccleston, C. (1994) "On the textuality of being", *Theory and Psychology*, 4/1, 85–103.

Sterling, M. M. & Bugental, J. F. T. (1993) "The meld experience in psychotherapy supervision", *Journal of Humanistic Psychology*, 33/2, 38–48.

Stiles, W. B. (1999) "Signs and voices in psychotherapy", *Psychotherapy Research*, 9, 1–21.

Stiles, W. B. & Glick, M. J. (2002) "Client-centered therapy with multi-voiced clients: Empathy with whom?", in J. C. Watson, R. N. Goldman & M. S. Warner (eds) *Client-Centered and Experiential Psychotherapy in the 21st Century: Advances in theory, research and practice* (pp.406–414), Llangarron, UK: PCCS Books.

Stone, H. & Winkelman, S. (1985) *Embracing Our Selves*, Marina del Ray, CA: Devorss & Co.

Strümpfel, U. & Goldman, R. (2002) "Contacting Gestalt therapy", in D. J. Cain (ed) *Humanistic Psychotherapies: Handbook of research and practice*, Washington, DC: APA.

Swinney, G. (1999) "A shamanic dream journey", in S. Krippner & S. R. Waldman (eds) *Dreamscaping*, Los Angeles: Roxbury Park.

Tart, C. (1986) *Waking Up: Overcoming the obstacles to human potential*, Boston: New Science Library.

Traeger, J., Daisley, J. & Willis, L. (2006) *Navigator: Men's development workbook* (2nd ed.), Stroud, UK: Hawthorn Press.

Valsiner, J. (2002) "Forms of dialogical relations and semiotic autoregulation within the self" *Theory and Psychology*, 12/2, 251–265.

Vargiu, J. G. (1974) "Psychosynthesis workbook: Subpersonalities", *Synthesis*, 1.

Verhofstadt-Denève, L. M. F. (2003) "The psychodramatical 'social atom method': Dialogical self in dialectical action", *Journal of Constructivist Psychology*, 16, 183–212.

Voloshinov, V. N. (1986) *Marxism and the Philosophy of Language*, Cambridge, MA: Harvard University Press.

Wake, L. (2007) *Neurolinguistic Therapy: A postmodern perspective*, Hove, UK: Routledge.

Wallace, W. (1898) *Prolegomena to the Logic of Hegel*, Oxford: Clarendon Press.

Warmoth, A. (1997) Personal communication.

Watkins, J. G. (1976) "Ego states and the problem of responsibility: A psychological analysis of the Patty Hearst case", *Journal of Psychiatry and Law*, Winter, 471–489.

Watkins, J. G. (1978a) *The Therapeutic Self*, New York: Human Sciences Press.

Watkins, J. G. (1978b) "Ego states and the problem of responsibility II: The case of Patricia W.", *Journal of Psychiatry and Law*, Winter, 519–535.

Watkins, J. G. (1984) "The Bianchi (LA 'Hillside Strangler') case: Sociopath or multiple personality?", *International Journal of Clinical and Experimental Hypnosis*, 32, 67–111.

Watkins, J. G. & Johnson, R. J. (1982) *We, the Divided Self*, New York: Irvington.

Watkins, J. G. & Watkins, H. H. (1986) "Hypnosis, multiple personality and ego states as altered states of consciousness", in B. B. Wolman & M. Ullman (eds) *Handbook of States of Consciousness*, New York: Van Nostrand Reinhold.

Watkins, M. (1986) *Invisible Guests*, Hillsdale, NJ: The Analytic Press.

Watson, J. C., Greenberg, L. S. & Lietaer, G. (1998) "The experiential paradigm unfolding: Relationship and experiencing in therapy", in L. S. Greenberg, J. C. Watson & G. Lietaer (eds) *Handbook of Experiential Psychotherapy*, New York: Guilford Press.

Weishaar, M. L. & Beck, A. T. (1986) "Cognitive therapy", in W. Dryden & W. Golden (eds) *Cognitive-Behavioural Approaches to Psychotherapy*, London: Harper & Row.

Wessler, R. L. (1986) "Conceptualizing cognitions in the cognitive-behavioural therapies", in W. Dryden & W. Golden (eds) *Cognitive-Behavioural Approaches to Psychotherapy*, London: Harper & Row.

West, W. (2000) "Supervision difficulties and dilemmas for counsellors around healing and spirituality", in B. Lawton & C. Feltham (eds) *Taking Supervision Forward: Dilemmas, insights and trends*, London: Sage.

White, M. & Epston, D. (1990) *Narrative Means to Therapeutic Ends*, New York: W. W. Norton.

Whitmore, D. (1999) "Supervision from a transpersonal context" (5 pages), Handout from course workshop on supervision, Psychosynthesis and Education Trust.

Whitmore, J. (2002) *Coaching for Professionals* (3rd ed.), London: Nicholas Brealey.

Whitmore, J. & Einzig, H. (2007) "Transpersonal coaching", in J. Passmore (ed) *Excellence in Coaching*, London: Kogan Page.

Wilber, K. (1981) *The Atman Project*, Wheaton, IL: Quest.

Wilber, K. (1983) *A Sociable God*, New York: McGraw-Hill.

Wilber, K. (1996) *A Brief History of Everything*, Boston: Shambhala.

Wilber, K. (1997) *The Eye of Spirit*, Boston: Shambhala.

Wilber, K. (2000a) *Integral Psychology*, Boston: Shambhala.

Wilber, K. (2000b) *Collected Works Vol. 7*, Boston: Shambhala.

Wilber, K. (2006) *Integral Spirituality*, Boston: Integral Books.

Wilber, K., Engler, J. & Brown, D. P. (1986) *Transformations of Consciousness*, Boston: New Science Library.

Wingard, B. (1998) "Introducing 'Sugar'", in C. White & D. Denborough (eds) *Introducing Narrative Therapy*, Adelaide, Australia: Dulwich Centre.

Winnicott, D. W. (1965) *The Maturational Processes and the Facilitating Environment*, London: Hogarth Press.

Wolf, A. & Kutash, I. L. (1986) "Psychoanalysis in groups", in I. L. Kutash & A. Wolf (eds) *Psychotherapist's Notebook*, San Francisco: Jossey-Bass.

Woolger, R. J. (1990) *Other Lives, Other Selves: A Jungian psychotherapist discovers past lives*, Wellingborough, UK: Crucible.

Wright, D. (1973) "Images of human nature underlying sociological theory: A review and synthesis", Annual Meeting of the American Sociological Association.

Yontef, G. (1993) *Awareness, Dialogue and Process*, Highland, NY: Gestalt Journal Press.

Yontef, G. (1997) "Supervision from a Gestalt therapy perspective", in C. E. Watkins (ed) *Handbook of Psychotherapy Supervision*, New York: John Wiley.

Young, J. E., Klosko, J. S. & Weishaar, M. E. (2003) *Schema Therapy: A practitioner's guide*, New York: Guilford Press.

Zimring, F. (2001) "Empathic understanding grows the person", in S. Haugh & T. Merry (eds) *Empathy (Rogers' Therapeutic Conditions Vol. 2)*, Ross-on-Wye, UK: PCCS Books.

Zinker, J. (1978) *Creative Process in Gestalt Therapy*, New York: Vintage Books.

Name index

Adi Da, 128
Adyashanti, 129, 137
Alderfer, C. P., 104
Alexander, 128
Allison, R., 69
Almaas, H. A., 5, 135, 137
Anderson, H., 87
Angus, L., 14, 99
Assagioli, R., 23, 48, 112, 136, 137
Augustine, St., 26, 27
Aurobindo, 118, 128
Avants, S. K., 18
Averill, J., 35

Baerveldt, C., 36
Bakhtin, M. M., 11, 12, 13, 14, 16, 23, 31
Baldwin, J. A., 29
Baldwin, M., 72
Balint, M., 22
Bandler, J., 72, 73
Bateson, G., 35
Baumgartner, P., 83
Beahrs, J. O., 16, 23, 68, 69, 94
Beck, A., 137
Beebe, J., 140
Beier, E. G., 138
Beisser, A., 107
Berger, 108
Berne, E., 14, 22, 50, 56, 57, 58, 59
Bernheim, 66
Biechonski, J., 76
Binet, A., 29
Blackstone, J., 131
Blatner, H., 51
Blomkvist, L. D., 52
Boa, F., 25
Bogart, V., 7, 14, 23, 76

Bohart, A., 137
Bolen, J. S., 47, 48, 137
Boorstein, S., 137
Bosanquet, 94
Boys, J. H., 69
Bozarth, 137
Bradford, G. K., 130, 131, 137
Braten, S., 21
Brazier, D., 129, 137
Bridges, S., 37
Bromberg, P., 8, 19, 20, 23
Brookes, C. E., 140
Brown, D. P., 128, 135
Brown, M. Y., 86, 119
Bruner, J., 12, 14
Bugental, J., 136, 127, 142
Burkitt, I., 45

Cameron, R., 142
Cantor, N., 23
Carlson, E. T., 27
Castenada, C., 54, 64
Chamberlain, D., 38
Charcot, M., 28, 43, 44, 66
Charles, R., 142
Chertok, L., 27, 28
Cinnirella, M., 143
Clarkson, P., 14, 56, 57, 81, 107, 140
Cobb, N., 141
Cohn, R., 108
Colsenet, 67
Combs, G., 9, 11, 23, 31, 139
Cooper, M., 6, 7, 24, 130
Corbett, L., 140, 141
Corbin, H., 5, 137, 141
Corsini, R. J., 32
Cortright, B., 118

Subject index